INDUSTRIAL
INCOME

PUBLISHED BY AVOCET BOOKS
www.avocetbooks.com

ISBNs: eBook   979-8-9890381-2-1
          Paperback   979-8-9890381-3-8

First Edition
BOOK PRODUCTION BY HAL CLIFFORD ASSOCIATES
www.hcabooks.com

INDUSTRIAL INCOME

The Investor's Guide for
Maximizing the Value of Commercial
Real Estate Leases

JUSTIN SMITH

DEDICATION

This book is dedicated to my family: Lindsay, Emmeline, and Annabelle. I am always in awe of the wonderful people you are and the opportunity that I have to love and support you.

CONTENTS

INTRODUCTION

IF YOU OWN INDUSTRIAL PROPERTY, YOU ARE A RISK-taker and the entrepreneur who wades through the marketplace of investors, lenders, attorneys, CPAs, brokers, and general contractors to leverage your time and talent to create value with your property investments. Your success hinges on your ability to craft a viable investment business plan and execute it despite constantly changing economic, legislative, regulatory, and credit cycles. The ramifications of your decisions directly impact the outcome of your bottom line. The buck stops with you. I wrote this book for you.

My first book details winning strategies and tactics for what manufacturers, distributors, third-party logistics firms, and all of their executive teams need to know when going through the industrial leasing process. This book will give you the framework to create a profitable industrial property portfolio, achieve the highest rent growth, attract the best credit tenants, optimize your property weighted average lease term (WALT), and reduce your overall leasing risk.

And you won't just learn mechanics in isolation. You'll learn how veteran practitioners think about the leasing process. You'll get insights into institutional investors' and leasing teams' mindsets. You'll gain a better understanding of how each member of the team supports one another. You will understand whom to work with, what to expect, and how to execute your plan.

WHY LISTEN TO ME

Over the last twenty years, I have worked alongside and across from the vast majority of the largest industrial institutional landlords in more than 600 real estate leases and sales in most primary markets in the United States. I've been the assistant, the apprentice, the junior, the midlevel partner, and the senior team leader. I've also partnered with senior partners throughout the state, country, continent, and globe, both within my firm and with other top-performing firms.

Additionally, I invest my capital in industrial property and implement these strategies regularly with my thirty tenants. My quest is to grow to one hundred tenants. I handle leasing with some of my properties, whereas, with others, I hire and work with leasing brokers. I invested with my fellow partners to purchase our office building and have gone on to invest in a dozen properties in a limited partnership capacity.

But I didn't want to rely solely on my experience to write this book. I wanted to draw from the robust well of talent within the industrial real estate marketplace, so I interviewed CEOs, chief investment officers, portfolio managers, asset managers, leasing managers, and construction managers from the top industrial investment firms nationwide. These interviews helped me to understand, on a deeper level, what investors need and want, and what they value in teammates throughout the process and within their portfolio.

Then I reached out to my top industrial landlord leasing colleagues across North America to better learn their best practices, understand their client relationships, and discover the ways they reduce friction throughout the process. This book is the result of that synthesis.

WHAT YOU WILL GET

As an industrial landlord, you are used to dealing with tenants that may move out in the middle of the night, damage your property, underinsure, late pay, no pay, cry poor, be angry, be aggressive, be belligerent, or disregard their commitments. You are used to handling construction challenges with contractors needing more labor, overcoming shortages of equipment and materials, and dealing with permitting delays and escalating costs. You know there are fewer ways for investments to succeed than opportunities for failure.

As a result of this complexity, you need to have a process that you can configure and customize if you are to grow and scale your investment platform. You cannot afford to be disorganized, inflexible, or miss opportunities. Each of those errors will result in poor performance, and in the property investment arena, poor performance means cash out of pocket, legal exposure, and frustration.

This guide provides entry-level investors with a simplified, repeatable process and high-level nuance for sophisticated and experienced investment firms. Whether you are a tight-knit family, high-net-worth investor, family office, developer, institutional investor, private equity firm, sovereign wealth fund, or real estate investment trustee, you will find structure and insights here to elevate your execution.

WHAT YOU WON'T GET

Sadly, I can't write everything there is to know about industrial real estate ownership in 50,000 words. Prior versions of this book covered acquisitions, operations, capital improvements, asset management, and dispositions. These topics alone are worthy of their own dedicated 50,000 words, so I will leave them for another day. If you are looking for a book on buying and selling commercial real estate, you'll have to look elsewhere or wait for me to get to that topic in future writing.

NEXT STEPS

Here I will give you a glimpse into the entire journey we will be taking together so that you can know where we will begin, the points along the way, and what the completed journey looks like.

In Chapter 1, you will learn what market dynamics to be aware of to understand the outside forces that impact your property.

In Chapter 2, you will learn that the leasing process starts by setting a baseline so that you understand all the pertinent facts needed to begin your journey.

In Chapter 3, you will think through who you will need on your team and how to lay out a timeline that will allow you to know how each moving piece of your property puzzle fits together.

In Chapter 4, you will be able to think through how to take a parallel path in leasing so that you are prepared for success whether you decide to renew your existing tenant or go to market to find a new tenant.

In Chapter 5, you will learn a framework you can use to understand what separates a good broker from a great broker to ensure you select the best one for you, your team, and your property.

In Chapter 6, we will go over broker listing agreements to ensure you and your broker's interests align.

In Chapter 7, you will see how to optimize your tour and proposal process to get started on the right footing.

In Chapter 8, we will review how to analyze tenants' credit, think through security deposits, and analyze lease economics.

In Chapter 9, we delve deep into lease contract negotiations and some of the most contentious and impactful lease sections that distance you from liability.

In Chapter 10, we review the addenda, exhibits, and work letters that will tailor the lease to your situation.

And finally, in Chapter 11, you'll learn how to transition from leasing into property management, tenant improvement, and property operations.

At this point, you can put your newfound experience to the test on your next property.

The famous proverb explains, "Every journey starts with one step." Next, you will take that first step into the market data to do the homework needed to create an informed opinion so that you can lead your team and start your negotiations from an informational advantage.

CHAPTER 1

MARKET FUNDAMENTALS

YIELD REPRESENTS THE RETURN ON INVESTED CAPITAL, and maximizing yield should be your primary objective. The leasing decisions you will make for your industrial property over the coming weeks and months will have an outsized effect on your ability to maximize yield over the next five to ten years. And to make the best possible leasing decisions, you must have a fundamental understanding of where yield comes from.

Astute investors will partition their yield into two components, yield from cash flow and yield from property sale. And a well-thought-out lease will seek to maximize both.

To maximize yield, you must understand the fundamental property and tenant markets to position and price your property to reach the highest-paying, best-credit tenant in the shortest possible time.

Think of the property market dynamics as the summary of what all industrial property investors are collectively experiencing in the marketplace. You can then think of the tenant market dynamics as the overall business environment for the industries that make up the collective tenant demand for all industrial properties.

When looking at these property and tenant dynamics, it is helpful to think of which dynamics are most relevant for your specific property type, size, and geography and then focus on the direction and magnitude of those statistics you are analyzing. You can then use this analysis to create a narrative that will form the basis for your strategy.

PROPERTY MARKET

Let's start with the property market first—namely, the concepts of rent growth, rent bumps, leasing concessions, vacancy rate, net absorption, weighted average lease term, sublease inventory, development pipeline, and construction. By reviewing each of these, relative to your property, you will know if your property is a turnkey gem; in a tight ascending market turnkey properties are priced at a premium, and you can push the rate. Or you may uncover that your property is one of many, in a descending market, where leasing concessions are averaging six months, and several projects are delivering this quarter.

RENT GROWTH

Rent growth is the holy grail for most industrial investors because it represents yield. Without rent growth, there is no return on capital through cash flow, and there is no return on capital through capitalized value upon resale.

Although leasing concessions, vacancy rate, net absorption, weighted average lease term, sublease inventory, development pipeline, and construction concessions are all essential market metrics to monitor, much of their purpose is to help instruct investors on how and when to grow rents.

Industrial investors have made fortunes based on the rent growth anomaly of 2020–2022. Not only does a one-and-a-half- to two-times rent increase have a material impact on the cash flow of an industrial asset, but it also has an outsized impact on the total value of the property.

Public REITs regularly report the rent growth they are achieving in their portfolios. In a 2023 earnings call, one major industrial REIT reported that even if they had no more future rent growth for the next three years, they would still experience a 35 percent growth rate embedded into their portfolio returns based on mark-to-market lease strategies alone.

To be clear, rent growth and rent bumps aren't everything, as cash flow, property resale proceeds, and yield proceeds are also materially affected by capital expenses, downtime, leasing commissions, and construction costs.

Rent growth results from vacancy, absorption, and development, so much so that we will delve into those separately later in this chapter. As an astute industrial real estate investor, you must minimize the lag between when rent growth is created within the overall market and when you capitalize on that rent growth within your property's next lease. In high-velocity and more significant marketplaces like Southern California, several data points will likely be available to understand when you are ready to market your property. In smaller markets, you may have to go more on gut and feel and work harder tracking down what available data exists.

U.S. RENT GROWTH

%, y/y

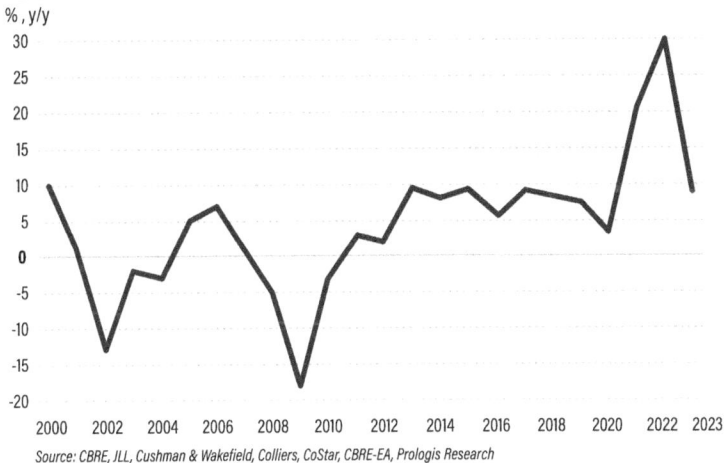

Source: CBRE, JLL, Cushman & Wakefield, Colliers, CoStar, CBRE-EA, Prologis Research

The industrial real estate cycle saw lease rates increase gradually for multiple years throughout the 2012–2020 years and then spike rapidly from 2020 to 2022. As a result, a new phenomenon occurred between investors and their brokers, where as soon as they signed a lease, another lease was signed at a higher rent. Rents ordinarily change over weeks, months, and quarters, not hours and days.

This extreme increase in velocity instantly upended the underpinning logic of all market participants and changed the rules for how leases were negotiated. Tactics of landlords marketing space

7

early by using the time running up to a vacancy to saturate the market with word of the vacancy halted, and landlords began waiting until the last moment to market and negotiate lease opportunities to capture the highest lease rate possible to capitalize on the daily increasing rates. Absent this anomaly of demand, marketing and negotiation methods will go back and evolve into new future strategies to adapt to new dynamics.

One institutional investor I interviewed echoed what most experienced during that time: "We were constantly looking at data, reviewing new lease comps every week, and wondering if we've peaked. We pondered if we could reach for a few more cents per square foot per month. Lease comps in the leasing market are everything. If you aren't up to speed on lease comps weekly, you are falling behind with the market."

Regarding rent growth, it is helpful to segment your data and look for rent growth dynamics of properties by similar size segment, ceiling height, and/or year built. Segmentation is a technique that will help you outperform your investor peers, as you will have a more refined understanding of your market segment. In contrast, most investors rely on general market data that may only partially apply to the property they need to lease.

RENT BUMPS

While rent growth is defined as the change in asking lease rates, rent increases, commonly known as "rent bumps," are the fixed annual rent increases negotiated for the term of a lease. Both are important in their regard, and the relationship between them is where more sophisticated investors maximize their returns.

Consumer price index (CPI) rental adjustments and a 2.5 percent annual rent increase were prevalent in lease contract negotiations when I entered the industry, fresh out of undergraduate school in 2004. After the recovery from the GFC, 3 percent annual increases became the unshakeable norm for 95 percent of all leases. During

2020–2022, however, we broke that standard and started writing leases with 3.5 to 6 percent annual increases.

You can see how powerful it is to keep tabs on rent growth and annual increases, as these two, in tandem, have enabled investors to increase their cash flow two to three times in the last five years. Frequently, the difference between two times and three times depended on how the investor and broker positioned the lease renewal, or the upcoming vacancy, to maximize the lease value.

LEASING CONCESSIONS

Leasing concessions are anything a landlord gives a tenant to induce them to lease the property. The most common leasing concessions are free rent, base rate reductions, and tenant improvements.

Increasingly, leasing concessions are calculated as free-rent equivalent, meaning that all concessions are calculated down to the dollar and communicated as free-rent equivalent. If you give a tenant two months of free rent, or one month of free rent and agree to build out extra office space, which costs the same amount as a month of rent, both scenarios boil down to the same amount of dollars given.

Another reason leasing concessions are most commonly taken as free rent is that, as an investor, you want the highest base lease rate possible because that is the basis of your NOI and the figure that will be used to calculate property value. In other words, you don't want to give a concession that has a lasting detrimental impact to monthly cash flow and capitalized value. You want to give a concession where the tenant receives the one-time benefit, and then it goes away without affecting the property's cash flow or value.

Add to that that you will likely renovate most of your property when turning it over from one tenant to another, and there is less need to give additional tenant improvement dollars.

However, knowing the leasing concessions that are market for your property is not easy because the information is private and not readily available. Leasing brokers know because they transact in the marketplace daily. And while leasing brokers may not know the decimal and how it is trending quarterly, they will have a practical sense of it. Public REITs discuss these figures in their earnings calls, but that information is only relevant to their business market. Lease comp databases like CompStack have 80 percent of that information, but you have to be an institutional landlord and pay for it or trade lease comps for that data, which leads you back to your broker. MLSs do not generally have reliable lease comp data and don't track concessions close enough to draw meaningful comparisons. When in doubt, ask your leasing broker.

VACANCY RATE

The vacancy rate is the first place to look to understand the real-time velocity of the leasing market. As the name implies, the vacancy rate describes the amount of space vacant out of the total inventory in a given market. Another way to think of vacancy rate is to think of what vacancy implies, which are other properties available for lease in the same market as your leasable property. The amount of vacancy will ultimately be the determining factor as to whether it is a landlord or tenant market. The nature of the landlord or tenant market will drive fluctuations in the market growth rate, rent bumps, leasing concessions, and more.

No set vacancy rate range applies uniformly across the country and across time. When I entered the business in 2004 in Southern California, the threshold for determining whether the market was a landlord or tenant market was 8 percent. If the vacancy rate was below that 8 percent, it was a landlord market. If it was above, it was a tenant market. That threshold continually decreased to roughly 3 percent, where it bottomed out and has gradually increased since then. However, that 3 percent figure applied uniquely to Southern California; comparatively at that time, it was 6 percent in Seattle. Your local market will have a different threshold.

It is not the actual number that holds any particular meaning; instead, the historical trend and direction of the numbers are where the significance lies. If the vacancy rate is below or above the historical trend, it is helpful to know by how much, for how long, how quickly it changed, and why. Then you can take that understanding of the past, learn about the current leasing state, and adjust your strategies and tactics based on your thoughts on the next quarter and twelve-month forecast.

Below is the national vacancy rate over the last eighteen years, as reported by Prologis Research. It is interesting to look back at this graph and think through what was happening during each period of time. What I covered in my first book, which most would argue has an outsized structural effect on the long-term lowering of the national vacancy rate, was the maturation of e-commerce.

U.S. VACANCY

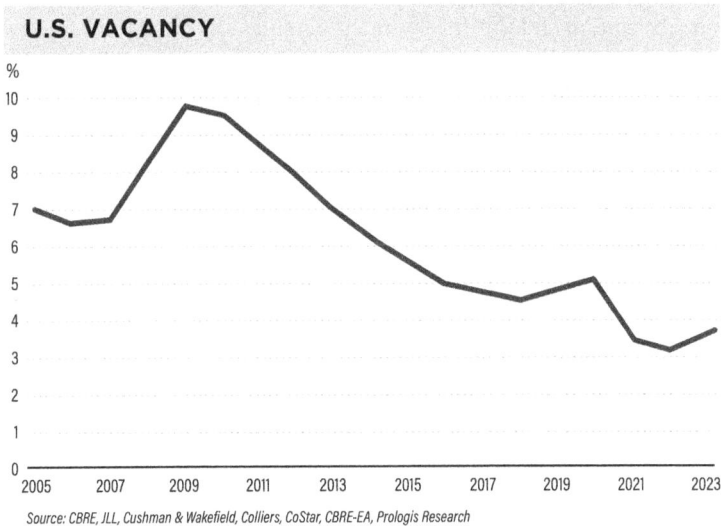

Source: CBRE, JLL, Cushman & Wakefield, Colliers, CoStar, CBRE-EA, Prologis Research

NET ABSORPTION

Think of net absorption as the opposite of vacancy. Absorption occurs due to a tenant moving into a once-vacant warehouse. Absorption refers to the number of square feet of properties leased from the total inventory.

The most common intervals of measuring absorption are quarterly and annually. You take the square footage of all the properties occupied during a specific period in comparison to the prior period and in relation to the total inventory. This metric does not factor in whether the property is new construction or a second-generation warehouse that a tenant vacated, but will tell you how in balance the supply-and-demand forces are in a given market and whether the tenants are growing and leasing additional space or shrinking and shedding space.

The chart below is the most concise way to understand the United States industrial market and see the relation between development pipeline and net absorption. What you are looking for here are the imbalances, like during 2008–2010 and 2020–2023. Both time frames disrupted the economy, yet the imbalance created between net absorption and the development pipeline was utterly different.

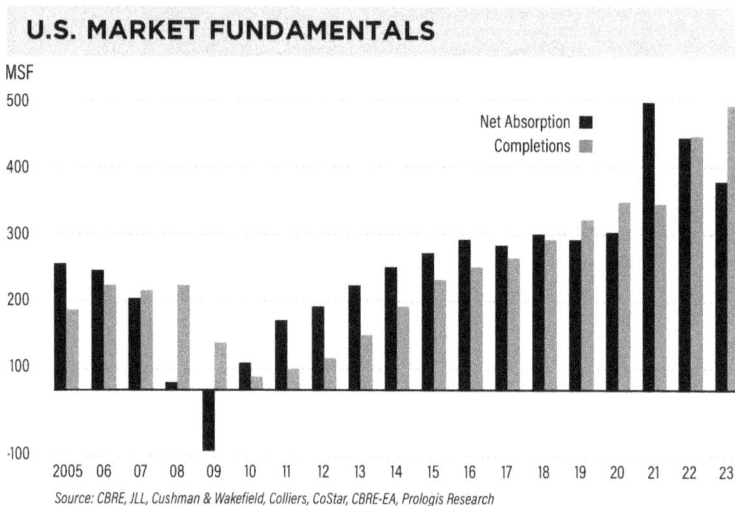

U.S. MARKET FUNDAMENTALS

MSF

Net Absorption ■
Completions ▨

Source: CBRE, JLL, Cushman & Wakefield, Colliers, CoStar, CBRE-EA, Prologis Research

At the time of this writing, we are in the middle of choppiness in the capital markets during historically rapid interest rate increases threatening to choke off the supply of new completions in 2024 and 2025. As a result of the capital market tumult, along with other factors like increasing moratoriums of new development at the city and county levels, many institutional investors are forecasting an acute shortage of new development availability in the near future.

WEIGHTED AVERAGE LEASE TERM (WALT)

WALT represents the length of lease terms that are being signed in a marketplace. Most investors are used to seeing WALT on offering memorandums (OMs) when looking at rent rolls and understanding how long it will take them to "get to the real estate"—meaning, how long it will take them to be able to get the building back so that they can add value to it and realize that value in lease up and/or sale. In leasing it is helpful to understand what WALT is normal in the marketplace because it will instruct you on how to adjust your lease term expectations when negotiating an LOI.

For example, in Orange County, California, the WALT for Class A industrial properties with thirty-feet clearance has ranged from 60 to 120 months at different times. Tenants often will lease for shorter lease terms when there is pressure on lease rates to decline, and during times of economic turmoil and uncertainty. If you know the trend line on leases is shortening, you can factor that into your strategy, your lease bumps, your TI concessions, and your capital expense budgets.

SUBLEASE AVAILABILITY

Tenants tend to sublease their spaces when they have excess space or when they have transitioned into a new space. Sublease listings also compete with direct listings and can have an effect on the overall leasing markets.

To be clear, sublease listings are not usually 100 percent comparable to new lease WALT, as some subleases will be for lease term lengths that finish out the original lease of the sublessor, and generally they are very short like month to month, year to year, or for less than three to five years in length. Sublease listings often will not come with turnkey office space or landlord funded and constructed tenant improvements. Sublease listings will usually be priced less than direct listings because the tenant who has the lease has an incentive to get the space off of their books as quickly as possible.

As a result, when sublease listings increase to the point that there are more coming onto the market than absorbing, not only do they provide alternative spaces for tenants to lease rather than directly absorbing vacant space directly from landlords, but they can accelerate lease rate reductions.

DEVELOPMENT PIPELINE

You'll want to review your market's development pipeline before going to market for lease because new projects coming to market will affect absorption and will have the potential to directly compete for the same tenants as your property.

In 2022, the United States had over 500 million square feet in the development pipeline. You can compare development pipeline data across different markets, during specific time periods, before and after the maturation of e-commerce, and for any category that is helpful to draw meaningful data for the analysis that is needed.

U.S. MARKET VACANCY RATE

If the currently unleased construction pipeline (365 MSF) delivered today without any absorption, the current market vacancy rate would increase to 5.9% — well below long-term average of 6.4%. Vacancy forecast for year-end 2023 is **4.0%**.

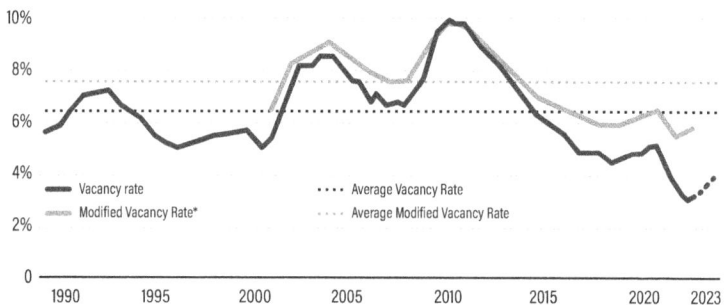

Legend:
- Vacancy rate
- Modified Vacancy Rate*
- Average Vacancy Rate
- Average Modified Vacancy Rate

* Modified Vacancy Rate reflects the addition of the unleased under construction pipeline. Pre-lease data available from 2000-2022.
Source: CBRE, JLL, Cushman & Wakefield, Colliers, CoStar, CBRE-EA, Prologis Research

For example, as the previous chart illustrates, with the elevated absorption levels in 2021 and 2022, vacancy rates pushed so low that even if no further demand took place and all of the completions were delivered on time, we still would be in a healthy and balanced market. This is a great example of how a public REIT used the cross section of vacancy, net absorption, and development pipeline to assess the risk of their overall portfolio.

WAREHOUSE MORATORIUMS ARE SPREADING

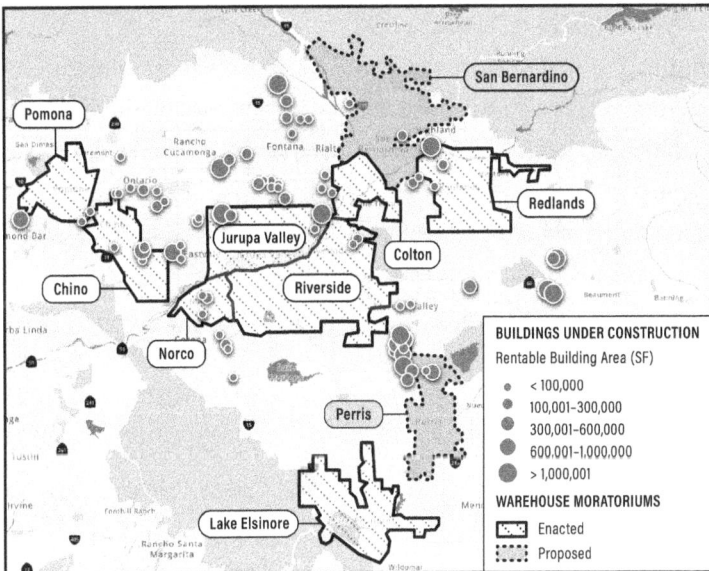

Source: CoStar, Prologis Research

Preleasing is another development-related metric that is important to monitor when leasing new construction. Preleasing represents the amount of new construction that is leased to tenants before the completion of construction. A lease signed before the completion of construction represents a lower lease-up risk for a developer and a milestone on the way toward completion of a project. Preleasing can increase and decrease based on leasing demand, as well as on perception, as many tenants will delay decisions if they perceive there to be lower prices in the future.

Knowing the cities' and counties' stance on development in your property's marketplace is also an important factor for the overall leasing strategy of your property. This is because if there are impediments to developing a new property, that will increase the lease rates and values of the existing building inventory and new projects that have already been entitled and permitted. The map from Prologis Research (see the previous page) shows the current level of warehouse moratoriums within the Inland Empire.

CONSTRUCTION COSTS

During the first half of my career, the availability and cost of building materials were a known and steady variable in most construction projects I encountered. But everything changed in 2020 when virtually every input that goes into a construction project increased in price and was in short supply. The following graph from Prologis charts these expenses.

WAREHOUSE CONSTRUCTION COST INDEX, U.S.

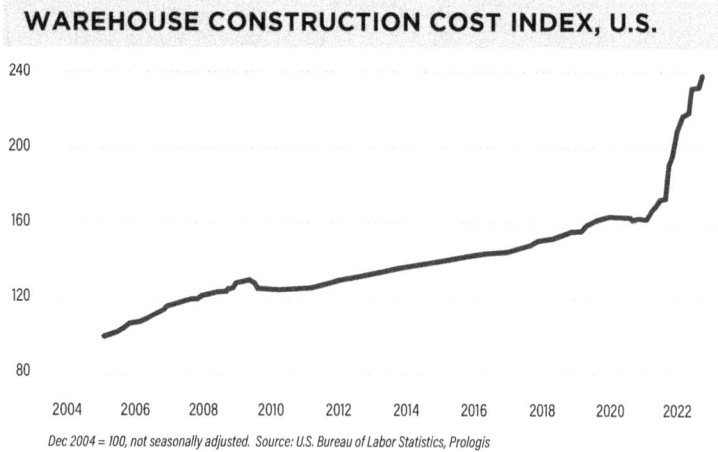

Dec 2004 = 100, not seasonally adjusted. Source: U.S. Bureau of Labor Statistics, Prologis

Construction costs (generally for either new construction or tenant improvements) are an integral part of the property market as they are the most significant expense item that is paid directly, or funded, by the investor. Not only does the price of construction matter, but the availability of materials is equally essential. During

2020–2022, the asset managers who achieved the best cash flow were often the asset managers who ordered all their dock equipment, HVAC units, and LED lights early. These asset managers saw the impending shortage of construction materials needed for their new developments and tenant improvements and took a proactive approach to mitigate risk. Mitigating risk in this regard comes with its own set of issues to navigate—namely, where you hold said building materials and the increased carrying cost to purchase them early.

ARCHITECTURAL BILLING INDEX (ABI)

Carlos Serra is Rexford Industrial Realty's Executive Vice President of Development and Construction with more than twenty-five years of experience, both domestically and internationally. He has led multiple business units within public mid/large-cap companies and private growth businesses. Carlos oversees various groups at Rexford and is part of the executive leadership team.

To explain how we can use the ABI to track construction costs, which was never more pressing than during the 2020–2022 market run-up, he says, "Most of the data on the development side is from lagging indicators. But the ABI, which stems from the American Institute of Architects (AIA), publishes a monthly survey of architects. The index uses the over/under fifty as a bellwether for shifting market sentiment in architectural billings. Thus, if there is a score over fifty, it reflects an increase in design workload. If it's below fifty, you have a decrease. The premise is if architectural billing levels are increasing, we would reasonably expect a corresponding increase in construction activity nine to twelve months later after the design process is complete, hence we can use the index as a leading indicator for likely construction activity, which will in turn impact the level of demand and construction cost escalation.

"A lagging indicator is the California Construction Cost Index (CCCI) published by the California Department of General Services.

You have to be very careful utilizing data points, though. For example, if you look at nationally published construction data, they are reflecting an increase of approximately 7 percent in 2021. However, in the same year, the CCCI showed an annual increase of 13 percent, covering multiple sectors, some of which actually declined during this period. As such, I would argue that industrial is probably 7–10 percent above even the CCCI levels, primarily because of the extraordinarily high industrial demand during this period. Other valuable tools for tracking construction costs are commodity pricing levels and construction unemployment rates. Over the next few years, we will likely see some drops in commodity pricing levels as supply chain issues dissipate, as well as an overall softening in construction costs escalation from the COVID peaks; however, labor shortages, and in particular skilled labor, will continue to ensure construction costs remain close to historical highs."

Carlos also helps clarify how construction costs and the ABI relate to leasing and yield: "The biggest challenge is the escalation where you can take a simplistic and conservative approach and escalate rental rates at 3 percent a year, which, in recent years, is understated. You can also escalate construction, but our challenge with our yields (returns) is that the rental rate escalation is far more sensitive than the construction escalation—simply because the rental rate is used to calculate net operating income (NOI) and is the numerator when calculating your yield versus the overall project costs (land + construction costs), which is the denominator in the calculation. It's a real challenge for all developers right now to get some kind of consensus because our costs, something that we underwrote at $10 million two years ago, will probably cost us $13 to $14 million today."

Now that we have a better understanding of the property market dynamics impacting the leasing environment, let's focus on industry- and economy-related aspects that affect the tenants in the market looking to lease industrial property.

TENANT MARKET DYNAMICS

Once you feel confident about your overall knowledge of the property market for the property you need to lease, you are best served to analyze the tenant market and the needs of tenants as they grow their businesses. In order to know your tenant base, you must understand the key drivers that keep them up at night, which in industrial real estate is labor, transportation, and inventory.

The tenant base of industrial real estate is highly diversified, with tenants ranging from logistics to manufacturing, retailers, life-science, automotive, aerospace, and even to general-contracting and service-based businesses. However, the common need for all these industries is suitable real estate, reliable and affordable labor, and efficient and resilient transportation.

Labor analytics can consist of a myriad of perspectives. Namely, though, the relevant lenses through which we can evaluate labor have to do with labor quality, labor availability, and labor costs. Each of these categories will then break down into further labor subcategories that you can focus on depending on the type of property you have to lease.

Transportation analytics relate to the importance of ports, intermodal rail, and national transportation infrastructure to your tenant demand. Then, similar to labor, this can further be refined into transportation quality, transportation availability, and transportation costs. These subcategories will be different for property near the ports versus property near intermodal stations versus smaller tertiary markets.

In the chart (see the next page), from Hickey & Associates, a leading international independent site selection firm, you can get a flavor for how c-level executives benchmark markets to compare the total cost structure of real estate, labor, and transportation expenses for a business owner looking to lease 750,000 square feet to service the West Coast. This is a great visual representation that can help you understand the decisions that your tenant base is making when they are evaluating your property.

ANNUAL COST BREAKDOWN

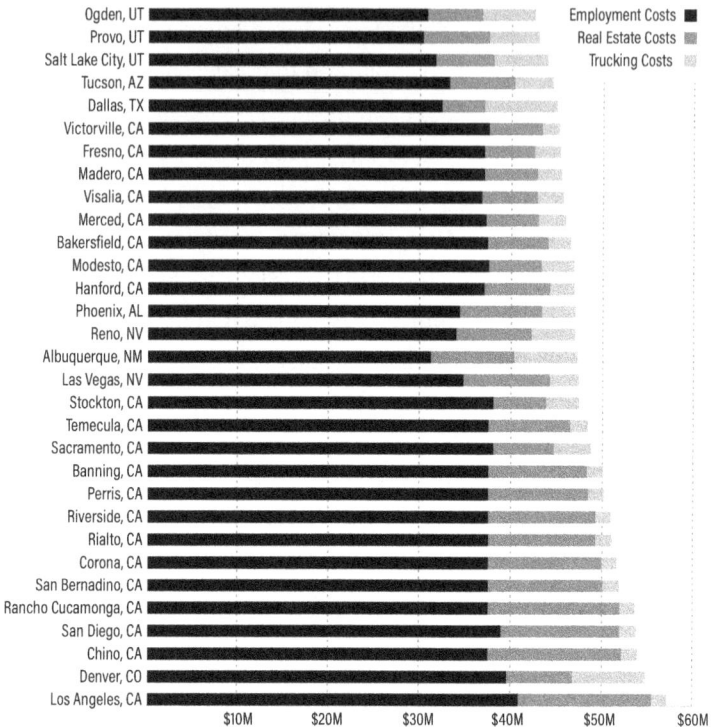

Cities (top to bottom): Ogden, UT; Provo, UT; Salt Lake City, UT; Tucson, AZ; Dallas, TX; Victorville, CA; Fresno, CA; Madero, CA; Visalia, CA; Merced, CA; Bakersfield, CA; Modesto, CA; Hanford, CA; Phoenix, AL; Reno, NV; Albuquerque, NM; Las Vegas, NV; Stockton, CA; Temecula, CA; Sacramento, CA; Banning, CA; Perris, CA; Riverside, CA; Rialto, CA; Corona, CA; San Bernardino, CA; Rancho Cucamonga, CA; San Diego, CA; Chino, CA; Denver, CO; Los Angeles, CA

Legend: Employment Costs; Real Estate Costs; Trucking Costs

X-axis: $10M, $20M, $30M, $40M, $50M, $60M

Source: ERI, CH Robinson, Cushman & Wakefield, JLL, CBRE, Colliers, Kidder Mathews, Hickey Analytics

LABOR

The state of the labor market cannot be underestimated when it comes to industrial real estate, as your tenants will only be able to grow when they can build a team that can execute their business plan. A cottage industry of consultants is available to analyze labor markets for executives to ensure they select the best site to locate their businesses. But what does this mean to you, the investor? While you may not have to hire a site selector or workforce consultant to map out wage rates, skilled and unskilled labor, and the labor cycles, it does mean that you need to be aware of how your property and your market stack up against competing properties' labor markets so you can position it to land the right tenant, at the right time, with the optimal terms; it is relevant to note that the larger your property, the larger the impact that labor may have.

The following studies and analyses give you an inside look into what prospective tenants are doing to choose the right property to lease for their operations. You want to know how your property's location compares to others to understand the strengths, weaknesses, opportunities, and threats, to position your property in the best light possible.

Starting with the Southern California marketplace, we get a high-level look at the subject markets from the 2023 Hickey study, A New Era in Site Selection, on the Inland Empire, which charts how each West Coast submarket compares.

WAREHOUSING MARKET OPERATIONS BENCHMARKING

	TOTAL INDEX	LABOR SUPPLY	MACRO SUPPLY	SKILLS SUPPLY	EDUCATION	EDUCATION ATTAINMENT	ENROLLMENT & GRADUATES	LABOR COST	MACRO LABOR COST	MEDIAN ANNUAL WAGE
THE INLAND EMPIRE	121%	151%	133%	188%	113%	106%	141%	90%	87%	93%
Dallas-Fort Worth-Arlington, TX	119%	134%	140%	142%	106%	96%	144%	104%	101%	107%
Phoenix-Mesa-Chandler, AZ	117%	132%	144%	138%	98%	98%	101%	102%	100%	103%
Las Vegas-Henderson-Paradise, NV	106%	113%	124%	105%	106%	111%	85%	100%	102%	98%
Stockton, CA	100%	108%	82%	139%	99%	115%	36%	92%	91%	92%
Los Angeles-Long Beach-Anaheim, CA	98%	122%	120%	134%	104%	88%	164%	75%	63%	86%
Yuma, AZ	97%	77%	99%	50%	86%	99%	33%	118%	128%	108%
Denver-Aurora-Lakewood, CO	95%	104%	120%	94%	92%	93%	92%	85%	80%	91%
Bakersfield, CA 95%	95%	82%	79%	79%	94%	107%	44%	102%	111%	94%
Tucson, AZ	92%	70%	66%	61%	97%	96%	104%	113%	114%	112%
Reno, NV	91%	85%	66%	101%	92%	100%	59%	97%	92%	101%
Salt Lake City, UT	90%	81%	68%	83%	100%	101%	96%	100%	91%	108%
Visalia, CA	90%	73%	69%	71%	87%	100%	38%	106%	110%	102%
Fresno, CA	90%	79%	77%	76%	87%	94%	59%	100%	105%	96%
St. George, UT	88%	68%	64%	61%	91%	103%	44%	109%	105%	112%
El Centro, CA	88%	67%	72%	52%	86%	97%	45%	108%	121%	96%
Sacramento-Roseville-Folsom, CA	88%	91%	95%	87%	89%	95%	63%	85%	79%	91%
Merced, CA	88%	75%	82%	61%	86%	95%	50%	100%	106%	95%
Albuquerque, NM	87%	62%	60%	49%	93%	104%	45%	112%	114%	110%
Provo-Orem, UT	86%	70%	71%	55%	99%	87%	149%	102%	93%	112%
Modesto, CA	86%	75%	60%	78%	99%	113%	42%	96%	99%	94%
Ogden-Clearfield, UT	85%	68%	60%	60%	99%	108%	65%	103%	95%	111%
Hanford-Corcoran, CA	82%	61%	72%	38%	85%	97%	38%	102%	110%	95%
Madera, CA	77%	56%	53%	44%	83%	96%	32%	98%	100%	95%

Source: 2023 Hickey & Associates

Another way to compare labor markets is to use the U.S. Bureau of Labor Statistics (*https://www.bls.gov/*) to look at the overall labor statistics for your given region to then extrapolate the trend lines for what is likely to happen during your lease-up period. Here are the most helpful indices to review:

- Unemployment Rate, Seasonally Adjusted
- Nonfarm Payroll Employment, Non-Seasonally Adjusted, 12-Month Percentage Change
- Trade/Transportation/Utilities Employment and 12-Month Growth Rate
- Manufacturing Employment and 12-Month Growth Rate

TRANSPORTATION

External transportation dynamics in the port, intermodal terminals, and infrastructure projects will affect your tenants' internal ocean, air, and ground transportation strategies and real estate decisions as a result. The more you can have a fundamental understanding of what transportation-related aspects are most critical, to the area and type of property you are leasing, the more effective you will be at positioning your property in the best light possible for tenants with active requirements.

Jim Clewlow is the Chief Investment Officer of the eighth-largest US industrial real estate investment firm that owns over $16 billion of industrial real estate and logistics real estate. Jim explains the importance of focusing on ports and intermodal as his company has built its core investment thesis around this specific infrastructure. "We took our initial investment thesis, built around the two massive intermodal rail centers of Elwood and Joliet in Chicago, and with the leadership of California Public Employee Retirement System, transformed it by growing nationwide with a focus on where freight connects on either side of those intermodals. This focus allows us to connect with tenants and customers on both sides of the supply chain, as customers tend to operate facilities both at the ports and at major intermodal centers. This transformation has taken us to the ports of Los Angeles and Long Beach, Oakland, Seattle, Houston, Miami, Savannah, Charleston, and New Jersey, and now toward filling key logistics hubs in between."

The following map highlights the major ports and intermodal and highway infrastructure throughout the United States.

FREIGHT FLOWS: HIGHWAY, RAILROAD, WATERWAY

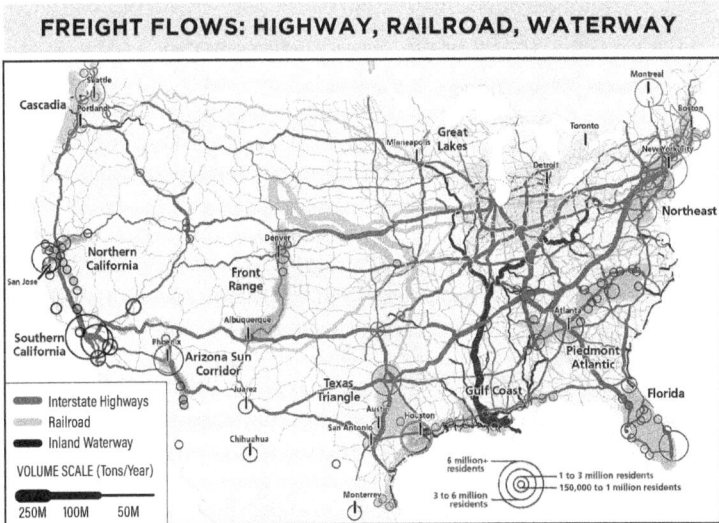

Source: Zeihan on Geopolitics, U.S. Department of Transportation, Federal Highway Administration, Freight Analysis Framework, 2012

When it comes to ports, intermodal, highways, and infrastructure, there are countless factors to which you could pay attention. The best tip I can give is to contextualize these factors based on your property characteristics and geography. It could be right next to the port or rail yard affected by tariffs, near a highway with a new overpass or off-ramp under construction, or near a new train station or proposed rail line. For Southern California we track ocean Container Spot Rates and Loaded Inbound twenty-foot equivalent units (TEU) because our market is very much integrated with the ports of Los Angeles and Long Beach. Container Spot Rates are the measure of expense to ship ocean containers from China to North America's West Coast, and the rates fluctuate based on supply-and-demand dynamics. Loaded Inbound TEU represents volume of inbound steel cargo containers, commonly used interchangeably on ships, trucks, and trains. Both highly affect the leasing demand for industrial property within Southern California.

It is important to think about what are the most impactful infrastructures in and around the area of your property, and how those projects' external factors weigh on the desirability of your property and the tenant demand.

For example, the labor union contract negotiations taking place on the West Coast ports, and subsequently the East Coast ports, are playing a material role in the quantity of freight that can move through local markets. This is the intersection of transportation, labor, and real estate. As a result, net absorption in East Coast port markets like Savannah and Charleston is increasing above their trend lines during the turmoil that is affecting the Los Angeles and Long Beach ports.

Suppose you have a property near the Port of Los Angeles. In that case, even though it is one of the largest ports in the world, adjacent to an excellent freeway system, six regional and international airports, and a considerable population, your property may be slightly less desirable to the global manufacturer who is importing parts for assembly or finished goods to the middle of the country. You might not push for the extra two cents and be happy with that $2.50 per square foot monthly / $30 per square foot annual lease rate. Or, hot off of the new labor contract signing on the West Coast and newly minted gridlock on the East Coast ports, you might be pickier about which tenant you lease, based on increased demand as tenants shift back to having their primary focus on moving goods through the West Coast ports.

The numerous imbalances caused during the 2020–2023 years led to ocean freight rates increasing four times, rail safety issues, trucker protests and shutting down border crossings, longshoremen strikes, labor disputes, and more. Each transportation shock had a ripple effect through different industrial markets. Paying attention to legislative, labor, and economic cycles within the transportation industry will give you a better understanding of its relationship to the tenants in your market.

TENANT DEMAND EXPANDED

So now that you can walk a mile in the shoes of your tenant, to understand what they look at when they are making a decision to lease an industrial property like yours, I'll leave you with two indices that you can use to take the temperature of leasing demand as a whole from a tenant perspective.

Graham Wahlberg, Vice President of Investment Management for Goodman (ASX: GMG.AX), a global industrial REIT based out of Sydney, Australia, with $8 billion and roughly 25 million square feet within the gateway markets of the United States, explains that after careful review and analysis of thirty-seven different economic indicators, the two highest-correlated ones are these:

- Leading Indicator: E-Commerce Retail Sales
- Real-Time Indicator: Real Freight Intermodal Traffic

This comes after reviewing the following:

- Rail Freight Intermodal Traffic
- E-Commerce Retail Sales
- Combined Transportation Services Index
- All Employees, Manufacturing
- Personal Consumption Expenditures
- Real Personal Consumption Expenditures
- Industrial Production: Total Index
- Industrial Production: Manufacturing (NAICS)
- Total Business Inventories
- Retailers Inventories
- Merchant Wholesalers Inventories
- Retail Inventories / Sales Ratio: General Merchandise Stores

- Retail Inventories: Retail Trade, Excluding Motor Vehicle and Parts Dealers
- Rail Freight Carloads
- Truck Tonnage Index
- Freight Transportation Services Index
- Merchant Wholesalers Sales
- Cass Freight Index: Expenditures
- Total Business Sales
- Consumer Price Index for All Urban Consumers: All Items in US City Average
- Retailers: Inventories to Sales Ratio
- Producer Price Index by Industry: Delivery and Warehouse Industries
- University of Michigan: Consumer Sentiment
- Cass Freight Index: Shipments
- Weekly Economic Index (Lewis-Mertens-Stock)
- Retail Sales: Warehouse Clubs and Superstores
- Total Construction Spending: Total Construction in the United States
- Rail Freight Intermodal Traffic
- Advance Retail Sales: Retail Trade
- Merchant Wholesalers, Except Manufacturers' Sales Branches and Offices: Durable Goods Inventories / Sales Ratio
- Industrial Production: Manufacturing: Nondurable Goods: Paperboard Container (NAICS = 32221)
- Producer Price Index by Industry: Lessors of Nonresidential Buildings (Except Miniwarehouses)
- New Privately Owned Housing Units Started: Total Units
- Retail Inventories / Sales Ratio: Furniture, Home Furnishings, Electronics, and Appliance Stores
- Personal Consumption Expenditures (PCE) Excluding Food and Energy (Chain-Type Price Index)
- Merchant Wholesalers: Inventories to Sales Ratio
- Total Business: Inventories to Sales Ratio

This data can be found on the Federal Reserve Economic Data website (*https://fred.stlouisfed.org/*).

Intuitively this makes sense in that bulk industrial properties now make up the majority of new development and an increasing proportion of the overall property inventory. E-commerce sales represent the action that creates the need for movement of goods, and the rail freight intermodal traffic figures represent the movement of those goods across the country after an order has been placed and needs to be fulfilled, replenished, and potentially returned.

KEY TAKEAWAYS

- Know your growth rate, rental bumps, vacancy rate, net absorption, and development pipeline over the trailing twelve months, and within the last three quarters for the market where your property is located. How have they changed? Why?
- Ascertain the current state of construction costs and availability of materials for the capital projects you have in your next twelve-month leasing cycle.
- Identify any pertinent ports, intermodal, highway, or infrastructure projects that most affect your property. Determine the duration, depth, and likely implications of said projects.
- Review the labor market to understand how it may drive your prospective tenant's site selection decisions.
- Look up figures for e-commerce retail sales and real freight intermodal traffic to see what the leading and real-time indicators are telling you about how the market is likely to evolve during your lease-up period.

NEXT STEPS

Now that you better understand the industrial real estate drivers that impact your property and its tenants, you can use this framework to contemplate your leasing strategy. This next chapter will help you understand what factors go into creating a strategy before we do a deep dive into lease tactics.

CHAPTER 2

SET A BASELINE

STRATEGIC COACH IS THE RECOGNIZED LEADER worldwide in entrepreneurial coaching, of which I've been a part for more than ten years. In Strategic Coach we meet with other high-performance entrepreneurs to transform our businesses every ninety days. One crucial exercise we start every workshop with is called The Moving Future(™), and it consists of three frameworks where we start by looking back at what we are proud of over the last quarter, reflect on what is giving us confidence in the present moment, and then shift our focus forward to what excites us about the future. This exercise provides clarity of intent based on morale, momentum, and motivation that entrepreneurs can use to identify the next five achievements that will multiply their success.

Look at setting a baseline in industrial leasing the same way. The idea here is that before taking action, it's important to take a moment to inventory the past, present, and future. This baseline exercise can be complex if it involves a portfolio of properties within a defined investment horizon, like leasing out the 211,000-square-foot, seven-building, small-bay portfolio my team sold to an institutional investor in the Inland Empire. Other times it can be straightforward, like with a West LA family office we have helped for more than ten years with half a dozen of their single-tenant warehouses, where they needed a young, hungry broker to invigorate their leasing process.

Regardless of a property's size and scope, impending vacancy generally means there is an opportunity to maximize the value of the property and cash-flow stream through strategic leasing and minimize the downtime or lost revenue stream from vacancy and suboptimal lease terms.

Setting a baseline for leasing ground-up construction takes different considerations than leasing existing buildings, as the entitlement and construction time is significantly longer. For second-generation buildings, we start with taking inventory of the current lease and helping investors exit their old lease to protect their interests and set them up for success in constructing improvements, capital expenditures, and lease execution.

SET A BASELINE

Graham Wahlberg, Vice President of Investment Management for Goodman, helps his firm set a baseline with all of their assets. "Every year, we go through a business planning process. Portfolio managers create expectations for the next year, create budgets for each asset within the portfolio, and target returns for the portfolio. Locally we go through every market, LA, Inland Empire, and Orange County, and underwrite a prototypical project based on our market leasing assumptions and valuations. As a result, our return expectations will adjust based on market cap rates and rent growth. This exercise sets the stage for how you will excel and invest in the coming year."

Carlos Serra eloquently explains the lens through which you can consider where your property and leasing strategy is on the risk-return spectrum. He explains, "Our sweet spot is value-add deals through repositioning an existing asset which has likely become functionally obsolescent over the years. This typically drives higher yields. However, you are inherently taking on increased risk due to more unknown site conditions, all of which can be mitigated by utilizing the right resources. Following repositions, ground-up deals would be the next highest yields where you arguably have slightly lower risk, followed by the lowest risk and lowest returns of newer stabilized assets. You need to know and mitigate the risk going into a project and understand how you will balance all three within your portfolio. It is important to note that the basic concept of yields discussed above only factors in the overall investment and the NOI. What is not factored in for this particular analysis is the timing of when the income is generated. This is a particularly important consideration concerning ground-up deals where you often need to navigate through an extensive entitlement and permitting plan, which can take months and years."

Most of the properties we sell to industrial investors are leased investments. These are properties that already have tenants in place. As a result, the first opportunity to help them with leasing is when their existing tenant's lease expires.

The lease expiration date is an inflection point where an existing tenant can remain in the property and sign a new lease or move out and move on to another property, leaving the investor's property vacant and needing a new tenant. Knowing that the process will go in one of two directions, we'll explore each direction, create a plan for either outcome, and, ideally, be in control of directing the outcome of your choosing.

Before this last real estate cycle, my motto was "fight vacancy like the plague." During the Great Financial Collapse of 2008, there were instances where we had 200,000-square-foot facilities in the heart of the most desirable part of Orange County, in Irvine, near John Wayne Airport, that we could not give away. The market velocity was anemic, the ownership was complex, and it stayed on the market for years. If the landlord had been able to negotiate a renewal for its existing tenant, even at less-than-ideal terms, it still would have been better than allowing the property to stay vacant.

Fast-forward to the peak of the following real estate cycle, and the opposite occurred. There had become an undersupply of property and an oversupply of tenants. For almost two years, kicking a tenant out of their space became optimal so you could re-lease the space for two or three times the rent to one of twenty tenants vying for it. After seeing more than an entire market cycle, I can appreciate that extending a current tenant customer is always worth exploring first.

Top industrial landlords and their leasing brokers stay in close touch with existing tenants during the lease term, which can help them understand their needs and adjust accordingly. That can help you determine what the tenant will need and how else you can accommodate them within your portfolio of properties. This closeness also allows you to estimate the terms your tenant might be willing to accept.

You'll want to be prepared to renew the lease or go to the market to find a new tenant, and go with the best approach that aligns with the overall property business plan. That will allow you to analyze the cash flow, capital outlay, and property value associated with either lease renewal or leasing to a new tenant.

LEASE REVIEW

In *Industrial Intelligence,* I discussed the need for tenants to review their leases when first considering whether they need to move out of or remain in their current space. As a landlord, starting the process with the original fully executed lease documents, amendments, addendums, memorandums, credit memos, construction documents, and any other documents related to your tenant is also important.

Before you do anything, review the existing lease with your property management to confirm:

- The tenant is current on all outstanding payments.
- There are no outstanding credits or debits to their account.
- The current monthly rent is the same as stipulated in the most current lease document.
- The lease expiration date
- Any lease option exercise dates
- Whether there is an outstanding CAM reconciliation
- Whether there are any hazardous substances that the tenant was using

- Whether there is any specialized equipment to remove that might require repair or replacement of portions of the slab or roof

Also, remember that you might not have written the lease on your property if the tenant was in place when you purchased it. Matthew Reynolds, Director in our Lee & Associates' Atlanta office and former Investment and Leasing Officer of EQT Exeter, explains, "When an investor has an ever-expanding portfolio, they inherit many leases. Not all of them are airtight. You should immediately pull the lease to understand your liability and exposure, the building systems and condition sections, and compare them with the physical space and the market as soon as possible."

Regarding lease options to renew clauses, Bob Andrews, Senior Vice President and Regional Manager responsible for the West Coast portfolio of Centerpoint Properties, says, "Many leases state that you cannot market the space for lease until the tenant's option window has closed." This is an excellent reminder that you want to engage your tenant before, during, and after the lease option window to understand their needs.

DeVonne Boler is a top institutional leasing manager for an institutional industrial property owner in the Atlanta region. DeVonne adds, "You want to ensure you have the right contact for the lease renewal, as with large companies and long periods, there can be turnover and transition. You would be surprised how often some tenants are unaware of when their lease expires. A good relationship with your tenant ensures you remain in contact even during personnel changes."

When tenants have options to renew the lease, it pays to know what they are entitled to and when their window is open and then closed. Is there a fair market value determination process in the lease option, and are there leasing concessions and tenant improvements that are allowed? It is a balance.

Would you rather have a tenant exercise an option to renew at market rate with no allowance for any concessions, or would you rather subject the tenant to the marketplace that may be a landlord's or tenant's market? Your approach will change with the cycle, and it is prudent to know how your tenant's lease option language compares to the current market before proceeding.

PROPERTY CONDITION

Next, you should form a realistic understanding of the property's condition. Ideally, you should schedule a walk-through to have your team see the property's condition with their own eyes. That allows you to:

1. Make sure that you are maintaining, repairing, and replacing all of the necessary items that will keep the property in good working order and in a manner that maximizes the property's value.

2. Have an honest assessment of your cash outlay for renovating the property if additional renovations are necessary to get the property back into rent-ready condition.

Why is this important? If you maintain the property in first-class condition, you can be confident that you can lease it should you need to and can then take a slightly more aggressive approach with your existing tenant. If the property condition is poor and the existing tenant is responsible for returning it to snuff, you want to know that and factor that into the negotiation. Furthermore, some high-net-worth landlords who are cash-flow conscious might be inclined to forgo a significant investment in upgrading the property. Instead, they find that kicking the can by renewing the tenant allows them to keep the cash flowing and delay the next considerable capital expense.

REVIEW THE MARKET

Now is the time to take a moment to appraise your property by asking your broker for a Broker's Opinion of Value. The idea here is that you should know how the existing lease affects your property's value, in contrast to a lease to a new tenant at market rates or redeveloping the property. That can help hone your property investment strategy so that the next lease you put into place is consistent with your long-term objectives.

A Broker's Opinion of Value (BOV) is provided to you by a trusted broker who gives you a real-time assessment of your property's value for lease or sale. There is no standard format for a BOV; however, the general idea is that it should, at a minimum, mirror the methods an appraiser uses in an appraisal consisting of three basic components: the market approach, the income approach, and the replacement approach.

The market approach compares lease rates and sale prices for directly comparable properties and often makes adjustments to account for each property's unique characteristics to make an apples-to-apples comparison. Standard features that have a material impact on value in industrial real estate are the warehouse's clear height, the quantity or orientation of dock-high loading doors and grade-level loading doors, the type of fire sprinklers, the quantity and quality of office space, the truck court depth, and yard space. Here you will be reviewing four sets of data: available for lease, recently leased, available for sale, and recently sold.

The income approach is similar to the market approach in deriving from comparisons. Still, it looks at value based on the property's net operating income (NOI) and the cap rate appropriate for the particular property type. The primary value in considering the income approach is that you can compare the value of the property vacant versus fully leased. Secondarily, you'll gain an enhanced perspective on the market cap rates for your property and better understand how they relate to interest rates and cap rates of other suitable investments and asset classes.

The replacement approach used to be less common than the other two because most major metropolitan service areas (MSAs) had available land within their urban or suburban core to build. As a result, it was unlikely to tear down an existing property to build anew. Over the last five years, however, we have seen a dramatic increase in the need for ground-up development due to the steep increase in tenant demand, which caused a two- to three-times increase in lease rate. This lease rate increase created enough incentive to tear down older facilities, and then replace them with more efficient and valuable modern warehouses. Utilizing the replacement approach can help you understand the cost of building a new warehouse, the comparable lease rate for the new warehouse, and the commensurate value of the new warehouse vacant and when leased.

Best-in-class brokers can provide additional insight into their BOV, synthesizing the information into actionable items that give you a competitive advantage. Such additional sections include the following:

- Product Market Fit: Does this property fit into the greater submarket inventory where it will continue to lease successfully?
- Review Supply & Demand Drivers: Including vacancy rates, net absorption, and development pipeline.
- SWOT Analysis: Perform a strengths, weakness, opportunities, and threats (SWOT) analysis that goes into the qualitative and quantitative aspects of the property.
- Return on Investment Analysis: Create an improvement list for the property, a realistic ballpark of said improvements expense. Then communicate how those improvements directly correspond to the value in faster lease up to better credit tenants at a higher rate and know what that higher rate translates into in terms of property value.

- Real Estate Cycle Discussion: Become keenly aware of what stage of the real estate cycle you can and should weigh heavily on how to approach the market. Although it is unlikely that anybody can accurately predict when markets will reach their peak or trough, your broker should have a sense of shifts in the market sentiment that can help prepare for the inflection point within the current market stage.
- Data Analysis: The burgeoning opportunity to include data analysis is in its infancy within commercial real estate. Increasingly, investors and brokers have access to a wide variety of data sources to understand property market trends better. Overlay the property market data with debt, equity, economic, and political data to create meaningful analysis and insights.
- Legislation Updates: A BOV is another opportunity for a broker to differentiate by providing insight on pending legislation on the city, county, state, or national level that has implications for your property. The pending legislature might include a future moratorium on development, impending additional taxes, future needs for CUPs for specific uses, repealing property tax protection, clean air measures, or transfer taxes.
- Operating Expense Review: This is an opportunity for your broker to look at gross rents versus net rents and inform you of how to factor your operating expenses into your overall pricing strategy.
- Marketing Plan: The highest-achieving brokers will then detail for investors their marketing plan for how they are going to achieve the results in attaining the optimal tenant for the property. We'll go through this in greater detail in the Broker Selection section of chapter 6.

For all the investors going through the 2020–2022 market cycle, you would be wise to ask what Rob Neal of Hager Pacific Properties asked me in our *Industrial Insights* podcast episode: "Is this time different?" Or, as Bill Shoppoff of Shoppoff Groups says, "I've been in this game, on both sides of the market cycle, to know that there will be a shift to a tenant's market someday, and then it will come back to a landlord's market. Whenever I hear myself starting to say it differently, I look back to the mirror and remind myself, maybe this is a frothy time in the market, and you should be happy for your time with the advantage."

And a review of the market isn't just rates and availability. Devin Barnwell is the Managing Partner and Head of Portfolio Management for Brookfield Properties, which owns over 40 million square feet of logistics space, with a portfolio of over 270 warehouse, distribution, and cold storage properties with 42 million square feet in the development pipeline. Devin explains, "My responsibility is to manage risk at the portfolio level while examining each property and lease to think through how the assets will perform in the next market cycle. Assessing assets with the market cycle in mind allows you to rebalance the portfolio ahead of inflection points."

REVIEW PROPERTY PORTFOLIO

The more properties in your portfolio, the more you should be keenly aware of your rent roll and know other properties you may have, or already have, available that might fit your existing customer. The next best thing after renewing your existing tenant is keeping them within your portfolio so that you can continue accommodating their needs. While it is rare that you will own the next best property of your current customer at the exact time they need it, it is worth exploring if it is possible to line up the right property.

The larger your property portfolio, the more opportunity there is to continue serving your customers wherever they do business. An excellent example is Nicole Welch, Managing Director of Western

Region for Clarion Partners LLC, which manages an extensive national industrial portfolio. "We have a large national industrial portfolio as a company. When you have a broad portfolio nationally and internationally, you must have an enhanced focus on service to your tenants across markets. We spend a lot of time with real estate decision-makers, be it heads of operations, heads of real estate, or CEO and CFO level executives checking in, asking about their business plans and where they see growth opportunities. If we have product in that market, or if we are developing product in that market, we would love to be able to accommodate them. Nothing is better than getting ahead of requirements when you can. So much of this comes from relationship building and having someone internally who owns this role and can focus directly on it. And building on that, it is even better to have your internal communication systems and CRMs dialed in so you can better communicate each need to best direct it to the appropriate parties for action."

Shawn Clark, President of CRG, one of the most prominent industrial developers that have built over 210 million square feet worth $13 billion explains that "within our portfolio, we have real-time tenant data. And when you come up to the end of the lease, you can find a solution for that user somewhere else within your portfolio. This insight has been a pivotal part of our transformation from a real estate development company to a true real estate investment company."

This same lesson applies to properties you are looking to build or acquire. Having a "tenant in tow" is powerful as it allows you to size up acquisitions, knowing you already have a customer that could lease it. This "tenant in tow" can also lead to better acquisition terms that you can offer, better financing if you already have a lease ready to execute on a property you bring your lender, and better customer relations in that your tenant now knows that you are taking their future needs into account when looking for new properties for your portfolio. The largest industrial investors have internal teams focused purely on existing customer needs to leverage this opportunity.

Knowing and reviewing your portfolio will also help you understand if it's time to consider a disposition. Devin Barnwell of Brookfield says, "I've been through real estate cycles and know trees don't grow to the sky. I am a very calculated risk-taker, so when I see the team stretching into a market or product type that feels questionable if the market turns, I ask probing questions and make sure we consider what happens when the growth stops."

OPERATING EXPENSES

The three biggest operating expense (OpEx) line items are real estate taxes, insurance, and common area maintenance (CAM). Taking a moment to double-check your OpEx serves a few purposes.

Firstly, you want to make sure they are correct. It is not uncommon to forget to update them, communicate the update, or overlook this if you are not an institutional investor who spends considerable time creating, reviewing, and recasting budgets.

Secondly, you want to know how you stack up to the market. If your OpEx is higher than the market, you'll want to factor that into your lease rate to make a compelling offer to your existing tenant. If your OpEx is high, you might also have a more difficult time releasing the property to a new tenant and, as a result, favor a lease renewal.

Lastly, you might be surprised to find that they have increased dramatically. From 2019 to 2022, operating expense increases range from 5 percent to as much as 44 percent.

One area that you can likely improve is how you communicate the operating expenses to your brokers. They must factor the operating expense into your asking rate to ensure a competitive gross rate. Not only that, but they will have to communicate the breakdown of expenses, and the historical trends of the expenses, adjust those numbers as new budgets come out, and ensure that the lease is consistent with the lease document.

EQUITY & DEBT CONSIDERATIONS

Capital partners and lenders are important factors in your leasing strategies for the property. Public companies, REITs, private equity funds, family offices, and high-net-worth investors have specific stakeholders and fiduciary obligations that I will not discuss here. Most of the time, equity considerations involve ensuring alignment before charting a course to a future property outcome.

Joonas Partanen, Head of West Coast Operations with Brookfield Properties, contextualizes aligning for us as part of this fits into their annual business planning. "In a typical year, we start our business planning and budgeting in July and complete the property level and portfolio level market by mid-September. This multilevel planning allows us to roll up to our parent company and have our business plan updated by late November. That means we start early with our business plan, property-level budgets, operating expense, capital leasing assumptions, and high-level disposition assumptions. Then we go into rate forecasting every quarter, tweaking our market trends, leasing, and capital assumptions. This forecasting is to allow us to forecast go-forward returns. We have an open-ended fund with investors coming in every quarter, so our assumptions and valuations must be timely and accurate. Regarding debt, we negotiate with our lenders and oversee or coordinate all of the inspections our lenders require. We'll make sure that the current rolls are correct. We'll handle post-closing obligations, like immediate property repairs. Typically there is a major lease threshold, meaning that if we want to sign a new lease above that threshold, we need to get lender approval. Knowing these thresholds in advance for all assets is imperative so you can plan accordingly and know what you need to do promptly. During this business plan process, you will recognize which assets may be ripe for sale during the next year. This planning is important because not only are you going to prepare internally with your model, including pricing, returns, estimates, and assumptions, and working with your brokerage team, but you will also coordinate with your lenders, insurance, compliance, and management to make sure you are moving together."

While there are different strategies for enterprise, portfolio, and single-asset debt, the main takeaway is that all debt has a balance, a maturity date, and covenants. Before you decide to renew or release a property with equity partners or debt instruments, it is advisable to review your loan details.

Typical loan covenants are debt service coverage ratios, tenant improvement and leasing commission reserve requirements, pre-payment penalties, and reporting requirements. After reviewing these, you will want to compare your loan terms with your market lease assumptions to understand how your next lease will affect your ability to achieve your objectives.

Common problems that landlords encounter when going through this process include the following:

- Refinancing during a descending market cycle that requires an additional capital contribution.
- Not having enough cash reserves to provide the tenant improvement allowance and leasing commissions necessary to lease out their property.
- Not having enough cash reserves to replace the roof, HVAC units, and the asphalt or concrete within the parking lot or truck court.
- Having mismatched investment horizons and objectives within the ownership structure.
- Having a loan maturity and lease expiration mismatch that can hamper refinancing.

The sooner in the leasing process you uncover these issues, the better you can manage them. Use this inflection point of having the property potentially vacant to ensure you have thought through and discussed any issues with your equity and debt partners.

CAPITAL EXPENDITURES

Capital Expenditure (CapEx) items are one-time significant expenses related to the asset's value, like replacing major building systems such as roofs and HVAC units and renovating exteriors and common areas.

What's important to think about now is that you'll want to revisit the CapEx assumptions in your budget over the planned property hold period. If you do not regularly review your CapEx schedule and budget, like some private owners often neglect, the impending lease expiration of one of your existing tenants is cause to do so. Another primary reason is that the property will be vacant, which is more conducive to construction projects.

Improving and upgrading the building functionality is the best way to attract top-tier credit tenants. We'll spend chapter 4 thinking through what building upgrades have the most cost-effective impact on your ability to have the least downtime to find the best credit tenant with the highest and longest lease rate possible. You can then take your capital budget and ensure it aligns with your market leasing assumptions and overall property business plan.

Carlos Serra of Rexford Industrial succinctly states, "A frequent challenge in today's environment is planning around tenant renewals. We may run multiple scenarios to plan for a scrape and new development, a major reposition, or perhaps just basic paint and carpet. Irrespective, this planning (and associated costs) must take place months and sometimes years before the lease expiration. During the COVID period, rental rates were increasing rapidly, which meant that the later the lease could be executed, the more optimal the lease rate. However, this also meant that we would be further down the path in our planning process and spend before we were "pencils down."

Bob Thiergartner, Chief Investment Officer of Birtcher Anderson Davis, focuses on multi-tenant industrial property and explains where many legacy investors go wrong with capital expenditures. "Many assets are family-owned and, as a result, focus on cash flow. While a focus on cash flow is not wrong, this cash-flow focus often leads to a leasing strategy based on minimizing the number of capital expenses possible to maintain 100 percent occupancy. It makes total sense at first. But what happens is that if you maintain that strategy for twenty years, the project tends to fall behind both the market rent and the property condition and maintenance curve. We understand how rents increased and are willing to buy the difference between the old legacy rents and market rents. I look at it as if I'm buying a multiple over time, more like a corporate stock, than a cap rate. Additionally, when you can grow rents on these assets 20 to 30 percent under market and improve the property condition, you find a disproportionate increase in the revenue versus the expenses, improving your net operating income on these assets."

As Jack Cline, President of Lee & Associates' downtown Los Angeles office, explains: "Institutional owners focused on investment value are different from high-net-worth investors focused on cash flow, and they look at capital expenditures differently. We increasingly already have the right vendors for high-net-worth types. We know the value proposition in transforming their property by tearing down a portion of the building for trailer parking or adding additional dock high loading. We can show how lease economics will change as a result."

RESERVES

Your lender may mandate an impound account to track capital reserves, tenant improvements, and leasing commissions. You may fund capital reserves out of best practice. If you don't, you should. The real time to do this is when you acquire the property. At the very least, the annual budget and property vacancy is the next opportunity for you to update your capital reserves and fund them appropriately.

MARKET LEASING ASSUMPTIONS

You have gone through all of the pertinent aspects of your property as it sits today and relates to the future. It is time to refine your market leasing assumptions (MLAs). You may not have created market leasing assumptions for your property if you are a high-net-worth landlord. If you are an institutional investor, though, you most certainly have. Market leasing assumptions are the estimates you make when underwriting property acquisitions. The gold standard for underwriting is Argus Discounted Cash Flow (DCF), which will allow you to underwrite specific assets and entire portfolios and run scenarios for each potential acquisition and holding period. You can't underwrite without market leasing assumptions, as underwriting models factor in time and an investment horizon usually longer than the initial lease term.

Nicole Welch of Clarion Partners LLC aids her team in quality control when underwriting industrial acquisitions. She "really weighs in heavier on all of the MLAs during underwriting, and takes responsibility and ownership for being familiar with all of the comps in the market, knowing each specific deal point, including commissions, TIs, and free rent. Each lease expiration in your rent roll allows you to revise your business plan assumptions for the highest accuracy possible. We have to make sure that our team delivers on our assumptions."

Assumptions are usually updated each year and each quarter in institutional investors' models so that they can uphold their fiduciary obligation to their investors that they are being prudent with their capital. In your Broker's Opinion of Value, you will already have an estimate for the lease rate and the pros and cons of your property related to the competition. What you can now refine are the rest of your assumptions, such as these:

- Lease term
- Annual increases
- Downtime

- Rent abatement (free rent)
- Leasing commissions
- Tenant improvement allowance
- Reimbursable expenses
- Renewal percentage
- Capital expenses
- Lease inflation rate
- Expense inflation rate

I only scratch the surface of acquisitions underwriting here. To cover it fully might require its own book. For now, I'll assume that you have already purchased the property, underwrote it before purchasing it, made dozens of assumptions when purchasing it, and are looking to maximize your investment.

Update your market leasing assumptions to help you think through how your next lease will fit into the context of your investment horizon. It will allow you to forecast your property's performance and better identify when you have maximized value. The Inland Empire industrial market in Southern California during Q1 and Q2 of 2022 is a great example. Annual increases in lease contracts have gone from a 3 percent annual increase to 4 to 9 percent in a fixed fashion and can now sometimes be based on the Consumer Price Index (CPI) again. Those increases are just what is within the contract. In a marketplace where lease rates have escalated by 10 to 25 percent *per quarter*, keeping your finger on the pulse with annual escalations will allow you to understand if you should stretch for another year of the lease term, terminate your current tenant early to release the property at a higher rate, or sell your property because the market lease rates have peaked.

Not only will dialing in your MLAs help you with leasing, but it will also give you a sharper focus on acquisition opportunities as it will help you size up leasing value and add acquisitions faster and more accurately.

KEY TAKEAWAYS

- Get a full accounting of your present situation before you start taking action.
- Do you have all of the lease documentation? Are there any concerns within the contract?
- What is the property's present condition in relation to your expectations?
- What does the market look like for a new tenant for your property?
- Do you have any other properties that can accommodate your current tenant should they need to move?
- Are there any upcoming changes to your operating expenses?
- How do your lender and equity partners factor into your leasing decisions?
- What work is needed to make the property rent ready? What long-term capital investments are prudent to make at this juncture in time?
- What reserves have you set aside? What reserves should you set aside next?
- What are your market leasing assumptions going forward?
- Can and should you renew your existing tenant?

NEXT STEPS

In chapter 1, you learned about the industrial real estate marketplace. This chapter taught you how to prepare and inform yourself before starting the leasing process. If your existing tenant has an appetite to stay in the property and renew their lease, you now have the context to know what lease terms you would need to achieve for that lease renewal to be worthwhile. If your tenant seems likely to be moving out upon lease expiration, you will now have realistic expectations for what you can achieve in the marketplace. At this point, most investors are thinking:

- How can I maximize my cash flow?
- How can I minimize my cash outlay?
- What investment in the property will maximize my property's value?
- How long do I have to carry this property without a tenant?
- What tenant will maximize the value of my property?
- How do I maximize the return on my investors' capital?
- How do I maximize my refinance proceeds after signing the next lease?
- How does this lease affect my ability to sell the property and maximize proceeds?

We'll start with a Dan Sullivan question I learned from Strategic Coach to answer these questions. In three years, if you were to look back at your experience, what would have happened for this to be considered a success? Your answer to this will be invaluable for the next step of the process, selecting a leasing team and creating the timeline.

CHAPTER 3

TEAM & TIMELINE

IN THIS CHAPTER, WE'LL FOCUS ON FORMING THE right team and realistic timing expectations from when you start the leasing process to when the lease is signed and the wire sent.

On one 40,645 square-foot industrial property in Irvine, California, we represented a family office in the lease up of their newly acquired warehouse that was to undergo a full renovation from an antiquated property, which had been occupied by a robotics manufacturer for the last twenty years, into a Class A industrial property fit for a corporate headquarters or best-in-class manufacturing property.

With this landlord, we came onto the project one year in advance of being able to deliver the property in order to work with the landlord, asset manager, architect, and general contractor to schedule a full gut job of virtually every component piece of the property from the roof and HVAC units, down to the mezzanine, office space, and exterior facade.

With a tight-knit group of highly dedicated professionals, we were able to then create a robust marketing campaign to spend the time before vacancy saturating the marketplace with the benefits of locating their workforce within the property.

We were able to land one of the larger corporate neighbors to expand their manufacturing operations and customize our shell improvements to suit their needs. The customization of their interior tenant improvements necessitated collaboration between the asset manager, our listing team, the tenant broker, and the tenant to craft improvements that were in budget, with an acceptable timeline that allowed the landlord to deliver occupancy while giving the tenant time to further customize their space and move in their furniture, fixtures, and equipment.

One year later, the entire project team, consisting of all of the players for both the landlord and tenant, all got together to celebrate lunch in the warehouse to be able to enjoy a job well done. The landlord's property increased in value 75 percent thanks to having a long-term, credit tenant in place at a healthy rate during a time of cap rate compression. The tenant was able to secure a best-in-class property to grow their interests for a long time to come. Win-win!

TEAM

Jim Clewlow of Centerpoint Properties clarifies this for the commercial real estate industry when he says, "There are bad deals, and then they are bad partners. And I'd much rather have a bad deal than a bad partner. What you have to focus on here is alignment. When you have structural alignment with partners, good things tend to happen. We consciously decided to bring property management in-house for this exact reason. This in-house property management intention allows us to make the customer experience superior. We didn't want to detach from that, and although it can be more expensive to operate in this manner, it's worth it to ensure we're treating our customers right."

If you are reading this, you either wrote the check to buy your property that needs a new lease, or you are the asset manager responsible for your company's investment in your property. That means that the success or failure of the next lease is on your shoulders.

Thankfully you are not alone. The commercial real estate industry is known to have high-performing professionals dedicated to collaborating with you to ensure your success. At a minimum, your team should include a property manager, broker, real estate attorney, architect, and general contractor. It may also include an asset manager, construction manager, insurance broker, property tax protest consultant, and potentially an estate attorney. These professionals are all in addition to your lender, equity partner, shareholder, stockholder, family member, investment banker, tax attorney, and financial advisor. For this chapter, I'll focus on the common denominators and the team members tasked with doing the bulk of the heavy lifting.

The ideal real estate operator organization is one like Chicago's Centerpoint Properties. At the time of this writing, this Real Estate Investment Trust (REIT) is owned by California Public Employee Pension System (CalPERS), with roughly $4 billion invested in eighty-five industrial assets in Southern California and growing. What is impressive is how integrated their organization is regarding acquisitions and leasing.

Jim Clewlow, Chief Investment Officer for Centerpoint Properties, explains, "When it comes to our organization, we think of its structure like a smiley face. The eyes are the acquisitions and development part of our business, the nose is asset management responsible for leasing, and then the smile is the support team of executive management, legal, finance, accounting, IT, and risk management. Our team of seventy-five touches virtually every deal that we do. And thanks to our teams' construction background, there is no problem we cannot fix within our portfolio. We 'in-house' almost every aspect and function in the property investment life cycle other than brokerage. We listen intensely to our customers and our brokers. Sometimes brokers understand what our customers need before they do."

A well-oiled operation will allow you to maximize the opportunity of whatever market conditions you encounter when your property needs leasing. Anyone who has been through at least one full market cycle can tell you that a market in transition is challenging to time and execute.

One asset manager for a private equity real estate fund that we regularly work with explains, "You're solving for a range of outcomes, and you must be comfortable with the barbells (upside and downside) of those events. As the markets shift, you adjust your assumptions from the initial underwriting. As you get closer to the lease expiration, you're solving backward, beginning at the existing tenant, with a specific plan in mind. When we see a lease expiration coming, we have to think, "Is this a tenant that is in our best interest to keep?" If not, you must be ready to engage an architect and engineer. You have to know already how busy these professionals are. You have to know who is available and engage with them early so that they can get some construction drawings and pricing and have time to value engineer. And then we need time to get into the city for permits. And you have to be projecting out these timelines constantly. The intent is that whenever your tenant finishes their move out, you're ready and mobilized to start swinging hammers the day after it happens."

Managing your team on a real estate project is like conducting a symphony orchestra. But in this symphony, your musicians are property professionals, property managers, asset managers, brokers, attorneys, architects, general contractors, project managers, and construction managers.

TIMELINE

You can expect leasing to take three to twelve months and nine to twenty-four months for new construction, based on entitlements and construction. The overall timing depends on when the building is deliverable, your leasing strategy, capital projects, and market conditions. We'll hit each one in that order so you can craft a timeline you can count on and adjust as needed.

Matt Ehrlich leads the leasing efforts portfolio-wide at Rexford Industrial and explains how they out-plan their competition. "We budget every year, literally every single turnover cost that we're going to pay in connection with a lease. We budget downtime, term, rate, TI dollars, commissions, and any other space preparation costs. We'll leverage our sophisticated in-house design and construction management teams in parallel to ongoing lease negotiations across every single upcoming lease expiration, in most cases nine to twelve months from lease expiration. We prepare as-builts and space plan units to create budgets across each space to ensure that we are ready to add value well in advance of the contractual lease expiration date. This parallel path puts us in a position to accurately analyze where we need to be on each new and renewal lease transaction."

POSSESSION DATE

For an existing industrial property, the date you take possession back from the tenant is usually when your current tenant's lease expires. You should know this date. After speaking with your tenant, you will know if they plan to be out on time. I use the possession date here instead of the lease expiration date, as what matters is not when your tenant's lease expires but when they vacate the property. This conversation with your tenant will put you in the driver's seat for the renewal conversation with your tenant.

Mom-and-pop landlords of the past used to wait out their tenants and delay having difficult conversations about lease renewals in the hope that the tenant would wait too long and then have to renew or face stiff holdover penalties. This approach is no longer acceptable for an operator with a fiduciary obligation to invest other people's money. God bless you if you are the sole investor of your property and like leasing it that way. Otherwise, you need to drive the conversation to know what your tenant will do before it affects your cash flow, your ability to release the property, and the overall returns you deliver to your investors. In most cases, six to twelve months before the lease expiration date is the most appropriate time to initiate the dialogue with your tenant. Customer-centric landlords have an ongoing dialogue with their tenants and will know what the tenant is likely to need based on prior conversations.

If you gave your tenant options to renew (which I don't advise in most cases) or bought a property with a lease with an option to renew, you want to verify the contract notice dates. These dates, usually six to nine or nine to twelve months before the lease expiration, allow the tenant to give notice of their intent to exercise their lease extension. I'll review the option to renew in great detail in chapter 7.

The principle here is that you want to maximize your time to market the property and negotiate the best possible lease with the least possible downtime.

CAPITAL PROJECTS

Now, it's time to create a capital project timeline. This schedule might include only paint and carpet, or what many call a "make ready" or "clean and show," which is common for 1,000- to 3,000-square-foot multi-tenant business park units. However, you will need improvements for properties over 20,000 square feet. At a minimum, these renovations will involve modernizing the office space. You will commonly perform these capital projects during the transitioning of tenants:

- Roof replacements, membranes, and coatings
- HVAC replacements
- Fire sprinkler upgrades
- Dock-high loading expansion, equipment replacement, and upgrades
- Truck court paving
- Exterior facade upgrades
- Landscaping upgrades

These projects take time to design, permit, and construct. They also impact the leasing process, the tenant's perception of your project, and the lease rate. Here you will want to consider what improvements will increase the property's attractiveness and the return on the capital you are deploying into those improvements.

First, start with the date you regain possession from your existing tenant. When it comes to starting capital projects as it relates to the expiration date of your tenant, Bob Andrews of Centerpoint explains, "Generally, we are looking to start the capital projects that do not affect the tenant's operations, as soon as we know we are getting the building back. This foresight helps us jump on longer lead-time projects like new roofs, provided the installation does not interfere with the tenant's use of the space."

Second, create a rough estimate of when the upgrades and improvements will plan to complete so that your leasing broker can communicate that to brokers juggling their tenant client requirements. Don't forget to consider the time needed for permit processing, ordering, and delivering all materials. Buffer your time to account for the permitting process that involves plan checkers, county/city hours of operation, staff, inspectors, and a whole host of people who affect your timeline that is out of your control. Also, as you increase your portfolio across multiple cities, counties, states, and countries, you will find no uniform process among governmental agencies. This lack of uniformity can cause you to need more consultants and expeditors to understand each agency and to speed up the process.

Additionally, Matt Ehrlich warns, "Construction costs escalated massively during the 2020–2022 time frame, many GCs and subcontractors experienced difficulties in procuring labor, and city plan checkers were widely understaffed. The cascading effects make repositioning industrial properties even more difficult as you must prepare for more plan check comments and revisions than you're typically accustomed to."

Capital project timelines are the longest for merchant builders. Groups like Rockefeller Group, specializing in ground-up construction, must mesh their entitlement and vertical development timelines.

During this last 2020–2022 market cycle Jim Camp, Senior Managing Director of the company's West Region, explains, "Breaking down cost and time have become more separate. Not only do we have to project our costs in materials and commodities, but we also have to juggle raw materials delivery, which is very complex. Roof structures can take from fourteen to sixteen months. We had to contemplate ordering roof structures before knowing what our building would look like on certain projects. With shortages, you must get in the queue and commit. The same might go for dock levelers and switchgear. If you miss one part, you can't finish your project. During the long project cycles, you need to at least get to your Gross Maximum Price (GMP) with your contract to lock in your labor, material, and profit economics with your contractor so that you have controlled the cost side of your equation."

In closing, as John Quinn, Senior Regional Director of First Industrial, responsible for the firm's San Francisco Bay Area, California Central Valley, and Seattle markets, sums up eloquently about the overall intent of capital project timing, "Regarding new developments, you have to balance the needs of the project entitlement team with the market cycle and corporate account requirements. This balancing act means you want to be thoughtful about when you should be marketing your property and when to engage brokers' and tenants' proposals. Additionally, when it comes to existing assets, the last thing you want to do is miss a deal because you had an extra six months of downtime."

LEASING PROCESS

The leasing process starts with broker selection, signing a listing agreement, marketing campaign, LOIs, lease negotiation, and lease execution. This process can take weeks or months. The market cycle will disproportionately affect that timeline, as will the prospective tenant's "pace of play," the number of negotiated offers, your attorney's responsiveness in turn times, the type of contract, and travel schedules at a minimum. Chapters 5, 6, and 7 will go into each component of this process so that you can manage it with clarity of intent and purpose.

Even more important than the time it takes to get your leasing team onboard and active in the market is the execution of the leasing process. Joonas Partanen of Brookfield Properties, says, "The timing depends on the product type, geographic market, and economic cycle. And during the 2020–2022 market ramp-up, in a primary market like Los Angeles or the Inland Empire, you could almost wait until the last moment to lease a property to capture the new higher lease rate. Taking the appropriate lease-up time based on the market cycle is a real challenge. We understand that with larger properties come larger tenants that need time to plan for their occupancy. To balance a potential tenant's need with the growth of the lease rates in the market, we do our best to take market trends and use a growth factor to forecast lease rates, sometimes as far as six months in advance during that market cycle. That way, we could remain engaged in the marketplace and do our best to meet a potential moving start date while protecting our interests."

The takeaway is that you should have an estimate for the amount of time it takes for the overall leasing process, which you can layer into your overall timeline.

TENANT IMPROVEMENTS

We talked about capital projects above. But what about tenant improvements? For projects likely to have a tenant improvement component, it is helpful to understand that completing TIs is usually the last obstacle between you and cash flow. You might not know yet if your prospective tenant will require tenant improvements, but you should have a good idea if the nature of your property is likely to.

At best, you can negotiate a lease with a new tenant before your prior lease expires. When doing this, you can design, permit, and commence construction simultaneously with your property renovation. At worst, you may not be able to attract a tenant until you have completed your property's renovation and gone through the leasing process. Negotiations of TIs and construction pricing can bog this down.

The difference in these outcomes can often cost you six months of cash flow or more. A veteran leasing broker can guide you on all of this up front when consulting with you at the conception of a leasing assignment. Nicole Welch of Clarion Partners LLC summarizes this process: "It all starts with what kind of tenant improvements you are looking at. Will it be turnkey, or is it simply a tenant improvement allowance? This is all part of the negotiation. Most of the time, we develop with a developer and a GC. If it is a second-generation space, do we have contractors we are comfortable with from previous projects, or will we have a third-party or in-house construction manager on the project? It all depends on the size and scale of the TI. We competitively bid the project to three GCs, pick our GC, enter a guaranteed maximum price contract, and then have our head of construction take over the project. From here, you have your construction timeline and the critical path tied to the lease negotiation. You have to be as certain about delivery dates and how you define substantial completion. You must know what penalties are involved in all different types of delays. You must have mapped out everything related to your obligation to deliver the tenant improvement project and every material date along the way."

Now that you have a good estimate for when you will regain possession of the property, and the timing of capital projects, the leasing process, and tenant improvements, you can layer them into an overall project timeline. It is the creation of this timeline that can influence your overall leasing strategy. Now you are ready to take action.

KEY TAKEAWAYS

- Assemble a dynamic team of professionals that have the unique abilities you will need for leasing and construction.
- Engage your team early and often.
- Ask your network for referrals for professionals they know, like, and trust.
- Know your lease expiration date and verify when the tenant will actually be moving out. Then craft a schedule that is anchored to the date that you will regain possession of the property.
- Create a renovation plan so you are prepared to lease out the property to a new tenant.
- Split your capital projects into those that can be done during your tenant's occupancy and those that can only be completed after the property is vacant. Then lay out those projects in their logical order based on the possession date.
- Ask your broker for an expectation for how long it will take to lease the property. Then find a balance of early marketing time that allows you to engage the market while minimizing vacancy.
- Be mindful of the time it will take for the property to create cash flow if there are landlord-funded tenant improvements that will need to be constructed. Weigh the cost benefit of making the space as turnkey as possible to minimize the need for tenant improvements.
- Combine all your timing expectations into one timeline.

NEXT STEPS

Now you have laid the groundwork necessary to select a broker and engage the marketplace. This preparation will enable you to minimize surprises, prepare budgets, plan for design and permitting, and give your broker the ammunition that they will need to be successful when they are marketing your project and attracting tenants to the property.

CHAPTER 4

RENEW OR RE-TENANT

THE ACTION THAT YOU WILL TAKE NEXT IS LARGELY
determined by whether your existing tenant is interested in renewing their lease with you or if you already know that they are going
to vacate and you will go to market. If your tenant has no options to
renew the lease, you can influence the outcome to your benefit. I'll
break down insights for both instances to see how one influences
the other so that you can then dictate which direction you would
like to go.

We worked on a 43,000 square feet manufacturing property for a
high-net-worth client where we had leased his property to a defense
contractor that manufactures missiles. Three and a half years later
with eighteen months left on the lease contract, our client called us
and told us it was time to sell the property. Selling the property with
the remnants of a five-year lease in place was not valuable to the capital markets as we were halfway to peak in the current real estate cycle.

Here the landlord and our listing team devised a plan to work on
an early renewal with the tenant and the tenant's broker. The tenant
did not want to increase their lease rate any more than any tenant
wants to increase their lease rate, but they were entrenched in the
property with a long-standing manufacturing process in place that
included multiple chemical processes.

In this case, we were able to help the landlord recognize the
advantageous time in the market. We were then able to structure a
lease that convinced the manufacturing tenant to accept a new longer-term lease in exchange for replacing the roof and taking care
of a modest amount of exterior improvements, such as the replacement of trees that were planted too close to the tilt wall panels, new
asphalt, and repair and replacement of rusted-out handrails.

The result was a successful renewal of the tenant at a new higher lease rate, along with an improved property condition and image that allowed us to run a blind bidding process to then sell the property to the highest bidder that was looking for a credit tenant in a well-maintained property that would work well for a high-net-worth family looking to preserve their hard-earned wealth.

EXISTING TENANT LEASE RENEWAL

You can align your lease negotiations with your property goals when you know the value of a lease renewal compared to going to the market to find a new tenant.

TIMING

When you should approach your existing tenant depends on the size of the building, the market cycle, and your relationship with the tenant. In my first ten years in the business, you would approach tenants according to the following schedule:

- 1,000-square-foot tenants: Three to six months in advance
- 10,000-square-foot tenants: Six to nine months in advance
- 100,000-square-foot tenants: Nine to twelve months in advance
- 1,000,000-square-foot tenants: There were no such tenants

Fast-forward to the time of this writing, and from the 2020–2022 period, the schedule changed so that you would approach your tenants along the following schedule:

- 1,000-square-foot tenants: Thirty to sixty days in advance
- 10,000-square-foot tenants: Sixty to ninety days in advance
- 100,000-square-foot tenants: Three to six months in advance
- 1,000,000-square-foot tenants: Six to eighteen months in advance

"Whereas when the rental rates were escalating so quickly," Matt Ehrlich of Rexford Industrial explains, "we were holding off on having discussions that we want to have today, during the ramp-up in lease rates in Southern California industrial, rents would almost increase 3 percent per month or quarter. In that environment, it pays to wait."

The best time to approach your tenant will always be fluid and something you must assess with your team.

INPLACE RENTS VS. MARKET RENTS

A great place to start is by comparing the current in-place rent to the market rent and understanding the difference. The graph below provides you with insight on the largest gap between in-place rents and market rents in generations.

The larger the delta between in-place rents and market rents, the more you have to gain by going to market if your tenant does not renew their lease. When the dynamic is tilted this way, you may

LEASE MARK TO MARKET (MTM)

Several consecutive years of strong rent growth have produced a large gap between in-place and market rents in most markets. As a result, customers should expect substantial rent increases upon lease expiration.
Source: Prologis Research

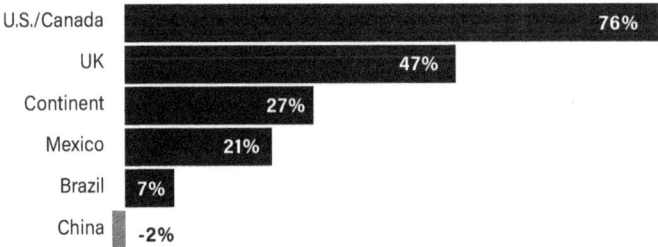

U.S./Canada	76%
UK	47%
Continent	27%
Mexico	21%
Brazil	7%
China	-2%

tend to wait longer to discuss lease renewals. The opposite is found during recessionary times when in-place rents are higher than market rents. In the descending market, you can often do "blend and extend" deals with your tenant, whereby you agree to blend their high in-place rents with the lower market rent in exchange for a longer term lease so you forgo vacancy, downtime, leasing expenses, and potentially an even lower lease rate.

RELATIONSHIPS

One of the best things you can do is consistently build your relationship with your tenant. This rapport cannot be overstated, as the better you understand them and their needs, the better you can serve your tenant and your internal team, contributing to everyone's overall success.

By building relationships with your tenants, you understand the role they play within the greater economy, across the country, within your portfolio, and within your individual properties. This understanding will give you a more holistic view, leading to better collaboration and decision-making.

Also, after 2020, corporate executives had to work more closely with their landlords to manage their internal supply chain disruptions. We saw how tenants benefitted from a healthy relationship with their landlords as they dealt with supply chain and lease rate escalation shocks.

To emphasize the importance of customer relationships, many landlords have created a customer solutions department dedicated to helping existing tenants to emphasize the importance of customer relationships. Emma Miller is a Vice President of Leasing with Link Logistics, established by Blackstone in 2019. Link Logistics is now the largest U.S.-only owner and operator of last-mile industrial real estate. "Enhancing our customer relationships is paramount for us," she explains. "We want to do our best to build and strengthen those relationships, particularly with customers who use our space in multiple locations across the country."

Jim Clewlow of Centerpoint Properties explains, "We know our tenants, brokers, and sellers extremely well, and we love to work with them repeatedly. Occasionally that leads to additional unexpected opportunities to work together, like the most recent 1.6 million-square-foot acquisition we made in the Inland Empire, thanks to our relationship. Building relationships is simple to understand, but executing over time takes time, effort, and thoughtfulness."

STICKINESS

Strategically, at the point in time when you will be preparing a renewal proposal, you will want to take a moment to contemplate the "stickiness" of your tenant. The idea here is to understand how vital the warehouse is to the tenant's business operations, how much investment they have put into the building, how disruptive it would be to relocate, and how costly it would be. In my first book, *Industrial Intelligence,* chapter 5, "Team & Timeline," I go through budgeting for the relocation of tenants as they have to factor in moving out of the current property, preparing the new property for move-in, and the cost of the move itself. If you have a rough order-of-magnitude estimate of whether it costs your tenant $10,000, $100,000, $1 million, or $10 million to relocate, you can use that to fine-tune your renewal approach.

You can also think of stickiness in terms of time. For example, let's say you have a tenant with a laboratory that took six months to build. If that tenant comes to you six months before their lease expiration and threatens to move unless they get below-market lease economics, you can interpret them as posturing or bluffing more than starting a direct negotiation at face value.

If you know the cost and the time necessary to relocate, you can be in a position to understand what truly matters and separate the signal from the noise in your negotiations. At the margin, this is usually the basis for a slightly higher lease rate, fewer concessions, and potentially a lengthier lease renewal term, should that be desirable.

THE RENEWAL DANCE

We have a saying in the brokerage business that tenants do not move to the same-size building to save money on their lease rate. To put it another way, there are rarely lateral moves.

The idea here is that the total cost of moving (i.e., the cost of moving out of an existing building, the cost of setting up a new facility, and the cost of the move itself) in dollars, hours, and stress is seldom worth it. Phantom renewal is the term that some brokers use to describe a tenant in the market acting as if they will lease a new property when all signs point to them returning to their existing landlord and trying to renegotiate. This strategy is so common, it's become predictable as part of the natural renewal dance.

If a tenant tells you that they are going to relocate, it helps to know why and what they need that is superior to their existing building. Having your broker be keenly aware of their dealings with the tenant broker can help you understand the likelihood of whether the tenant's interest is earnest or a negotiating ploy.

This uncertainty is why folks at Rexford Industrial run their renewal and leasing strategy in parallel, so not only will they be ready for the tenant renewal discussions, but they will also be in the driver's seat to execute their value-add strategy. In a rapidly ascending market, they've found that it can sometimes be better not to renew and to go ahead with the reposition if the market dynamics are in their favor.

Institutional industrial investment leasing manager DeVonne Boler explains, "It can be normal for tenants to go quiet during a lease renewal process. That quiet time is their time to research and contextualize their market renewal terms. They often come back to us with a broker who has educated them on the market, and then we can progress from there. Tenants not only need to know what buildings are leasing for, but they must also understand the consequences of moving their operation, labor, and transportation expenses. Many variables go into our tenant's decisions. A common occurrence can also be the internal decision-making of a large tenant between the local management and the corporate office. It is not uncommon to see a local GM understand the importance of a location, see the corporate office looking for expense reduction, and have the two work together to make a long-term decision."

During the 2020–2022 time frame, tenants would get increasingly emotional, frustrated, and sometimes angry as their monthly rent doubled or tripled, causing the tenants' businesses stress. It was the opposite during the GFC market of 2008–2010. It is imperative to have a market pulse when getting ready to do the renewal dance so that you know what song to play and understand your property's position in the broader marketplace. It all comes down to educating the client, understanding the leverage in each situation, and crafting a win-win scenario.

Sometimes the best thing you can do when you are wondering if your tenant will renew is to schedule a walk-through. Emma Miller at Link Logistics further explains, "We typically schedule walk-throughs 90 to 120 days from lease expiration. These walk-throughs prepare our team for future capital expense projects, ensure we meet our customer's needs, and start the conversation about whether they plan to renew their lease."

Even though the 2020–2022 run-up vacancy was beneficial because it allowed landlords to access the pool of new tenants that would pay significantly higher rents as the market normalizes, Jack Cline, President of Lee & Associates' downtown Los Angeles office, reminds us that sometimes "the devil that you know is better than the devil that you don't. Consider renewing your tenant as it is most often preferable and more advantageous than being subject to the winds of chance with a new tenant who may or may not prove to be a worthy replacement." Sage advice from a perennial top producer.

GO TO MARKET

If the result of your lease renewal negotiation is an impasse, or it is the natural time for your tenant to move on, it's time to prepare your team and your property to go to market.

The first step in going to market is to prepare to regain possession of your property. You will want to review your existing lease for the move-out condition language and then work with your property manager to coordinate walk-throughs. From there, you can be up front with your tenant about the condition in which they need to return the property and any potential consequences that would affect their security deposit return.

MOVE-OUT CONDITION

Just as tenants want their buildings in good condition when they move in, landlords want them in good condition when they get them back. Gone are the days of mom-and-pop landlords where tenants move out their furniture, fixtures, equipment, and all the warehouse products, and then flip the keys to the owner. Instead, institutional landlords have upped the ante for the move-out condition part of the industrial leasing game.

The industry now has a routine and robust set of conditions defining what's acceptable for move out. Here, the idea is that you must manage your asset as efficiently as possible, and setting up move-out condition boundaries for your tenant allows you to minimize revenue leakage represented in the renovation cost related to damage done by the prior tenant. Sample language might look like this:

Tenant shall surrender the Premises, at the time of the Expiration Date or earlier termination of this Lease, in a condition that shall include, without limitation, the following:

1. Lights: Office, warehouse, and exterior lights and ballasts must be fully operational with all bulbs functioning.

Replace broken light lenses with matching lenses. Ballast color should all be uniform (either all "cool" or all "warm").

2. Dock Levelers & Roll-Up Doors: Must be fully operational. Damaged panels must be replaced and painted to match. Replace all missing or damaged dock bumpers, dock levelers, Dok-loks, and Dok-lok lights.

3. Truck Doors, Dock Seals, and Awnings: Metal and fabric awnings must be free of damage and tears. Frames and fasteners must be secure and undamaged. Dock seals must be free of damage, operational, and securely fastened in place.

4. Warehouse Floors and Columns: Must be free of stains and swept with no racking bolts and other protrusions left on the floor. Bolts must be ground down or removed and patched with an appropriate epoxy filling; remove bolts with a gas torch. Repair cracks in the floor that are ¼" or greater with an epoxy sealer. Reseal any heavily scarred floor seal. Repair damaged or bent columns, bollards, railing, etc.

5. Tenant Installed Equipment & Wiring: Must be removed and space returned to original condition when originally leased (remove air lines, junction boxes, conduit, etc.). Security systems must be disarmed and removed with damage, if any, repaired. Remove phone systems and damage, if any.

6. Walls: All nails, shelves, and toggle bolts must be removed from walls. Holes must be professionally filled and sanded. Large damaged areas may require tape, bed, and sanding. Holes must not remain in either office or warehouse walls. Remove any sticky residue from placards or signs.

7. Roof: Remove any Tenant-installed equipment and have roof penetrations properly repaired by a licensed roofing contractor approved by Landlord. If roof maintenance is a Tenant's responsibility, then fix active leaks, and complete the most recent Landlord maintenance and repairs recommendations by a licensed roofing contractor approved by Landlord.

8. Signs: Remove all exterior Tenant signage, patch holes, fixings, and remediate and touch up paint to match, as necessary. Remove all door and window signs, and repair damage, if any.

9. Heating & Air Conditioning System: If maintenance of the HVAC equipment is a Tenant's responsibility, then submit a written report from a licensed contractor to the Landlord within the last two (2) months of the Term. The report must (i) state that all evaporative coolers and heaters within the warehouse are operational and safe and that the office HVAC system is also in good and safe operating condition, and (ii) set out detailed specifications of work necessary to put any equipment and installations into such condition. Complete all repairs/maintenance specified in the HVAC report by Tenant.

10. Painting: All touch-up painting must match the existing paint. Fully repaint scarred and damaged walls and rooms.

11. Doors: All interior and exterior personnel doors (for office and warehouse) must be in good appearance and fully operational, including fixtures, door closers, etc. Holes/scars in doors must be repaired and painted to match. Irreparable holes will require door replacement of matching and like-quality doors. Any signs or name placards on doors must be removed as well as any residue leftover from adhesion.

12. Ceiling Tiles: Replace any damaged or stained ceiling tiles in the office.

13. Overall Cleanliness: Clean windows, kitchens, and restrooms to full janitorial standard (i.e., strip/wax floors, sanitize toilets and sinks, clean under cabinets, exhaust fans must be operational, fixtures must be operational, etc.), professionally clean carpet, VCT floors require stripping and waxing, and remove all debris from office and warehouse areas. Remove all pallets and debris from the exterior of

the Premises. Do not temporarily store debris and trash outside of the Building. The parking lot must be swept and the dumpster removed. If appropriate, interior pest control treatment must be completed.

14. Building Systems: All building systems must be in good and safe working order (e.g., plumbing, electrical, fire alarms, intruder alarms, etc.). Provide certification of recent fire sprinkler inspection by a licensed company if a Tenant is responsible.

15. External: All landscaping, parking, and other external areas must be repaired as necessary if a Tenant's responsibility, including, without limitation, the removal of all debris and trash, remarking/repainting parking lots, repair/replacement of generic and emergency signage, resetting/replacing damaged curb stones, and replacing/repairing damaged gully grids and maintenance hole covers.

16. Upon Completion: Contact the Landlord's property manager to coordinate the date of turning off power and utilities, turning in keys, and obtaining the final Landlord Inspection of the Premises.

MOVE-OUT WALK-THROUGH

Your tenant's move-out condition language will guide you in what to look for during move-out walk-throughs. The next action step connected with this move-out condition language is to have your property manager schedule a walk-through thirty days from the lease expiration.

This walk-through will then go through each item to assess the current condition related to the lease language. In addition to the lease language, your property manager should provide a detailed tenant move-out requirements list so that the tenant can follow instructions provided to their facility service vendors. An example may look like this:

Exterior Premises/Entrance/Site:
- Clean storefront windows and entry.
- Clean exterior soffit, soffit lights (ensure proper working order), and entry floor surfaces.
- Remove any tenant-specific signage from the building, suite, monument, and property directory (patch/repaint as necessary to bring it back to pre-move-in condition).
- Remove any company-specific parking or loading/unloading sign designations.
- Remove all personal property from the exterior of the premises and the truck yard.
- Ensure all dock doors/drive-in doors, bumpers, dock lights, dock seals, and dock enclosures are all in good working order / fully operational and able to be secured. Dock seals and enclosures should be free of excessive wear/tear. Any damaged items shall be replaced and repainted to match existing ones.
- Dock levelers shall be properly maintained and in good working order.
- Remove any antennas or other receivers from the rooftop. If there are penetrations, have penetrations repaired by a qualified roofer that will maintain the building's existing roof warranty. Verify acceptable vendors with the Property Manager.
- Cancel trash pick-up services and have bins removed from the premises.
- Parking lot shall be cleaned after move-out.

Interior/Office:
- Transfer Utilities to Owner Entity name. Coordinate with the Property Manager.
- Transfer the security/burglar system monitoring account to the Owner Entity name. Transfer code to Property Manager.

- Transfer the Fire Alarm system to the Owner Entity name. Coordinate with the Property Manager.
- Remove all telco/data lines throughout (pulled back to the source). Replace data jacks in walls with blank cover plates. Patch/paint telco penetrations in the data room/closet. Replace damaged ceiling tiles.
- Patch all holes in walls/repaint.
- Replace any worn, stained, or cracked electrical outlet cover plates.
- Clean all window coverings. Ensure proper working order for all window coverings. Repair/replace any damaged blinds.
- Steam clean all carpets, wipe down all wall bases, clean and wax all VCT floor areas, and clean all hard flooring areas.
- Replace any stained/damaged ceiling tiles to match existing ones.
- Clean skylights (if applicable).
- Clean or repaint HVAC vents.
- Provide a written report from a licensed HVAC contractor within the last three months stating that all heating and cooling units within the office area are safe and operational.
- Verify that all office lights are fully operational with all bulbs and lamps working. Replace lights/ballasts throughout as necessary and clean fixtures. If the light fixture cover is "yellowed," it must be replaced.
- Fire extinguishers shall be charged and have current inspection tags.
- Verify all main doors/frames/hardware are in good working order. Leave keys in interior doors. If not available, provide re-keying of locks, and provide keys to the Property Manager.

Restrooms/Breakrooms:
- Clean/sanitize restroom walls/floors, fixtures, bath partitions, accessories, countertops, and mirrors. Leave stocked with paper goods and hand soap.

- Ensure proper operation of all faucets, sinks, toilets, showers, water heaters, soap dispensers, mop sinks, and floor drains.
- Clean bathroom ceiling exhaust fan/filter.
- Verify that all lighting is in good working order.

Warehouse:
- Patch all holes in walls. If damaged repairs are made to a painted demising wall, repaint the demising wall.
- Demolish any warehouse partitions. Bring back to pre-move-in condition.
- Remove all personal property.
- Remove debris, clean warehouse floors (including removing any grease/oil or other floor stains), and sweep & scrub the floor. The warehouse slab must be left clean.
- After the removal of racking, bolts should be shaved down to be flush with the slab. Any holes or significant cracks should be filled/repaired with MM80 epoxy.
- Remove signage/other items hanging from the ceiling.
- Sweep the underside of the roof to remove dirt, cobwebs, etc., as necessary.
- Any falling insulation should be re-stapled into place, and replace any missing ceiling insulation.
- Verify that all lights are fully operational with all bulbs and lamps working. Replace lights/ballasts throughout as necessary, and clean fixtures. If the light fixture cover is "yellowed," it must be replaced.
- Clean skylights (if applicable).
- Fire extinguishers shall be charged and have current inspection tags.
- Remove all aisle striping and aisle/storage numbers from the warehouse floor.
- Provide a written report from a licensed HVAC contractor within the last three months stating that all heating and

cooling units within the warehouse area are safe and operational. This includes warehouse heating units.

Other Items:
- Provide copies of HVAC maintenance records for the past year to the property manager.
- Provide copies of other building service records for the past year to the property manager.
- Provide Fire Department inspection records for the past year to the property manager.
- Provide fire sprinkler servicing agent records for the past year to the property manager.

If you do not already have the system in place for move-out condition and move-out requirements, it is important to remember that you will need to deliver the space to the tenant in the condition that you expect them to return it to you, wear and tear excepted.

By providing the property to the prior tenant in great condition, and then maintaining high standards for the tenants' maintenance, you create an opportunity to level up your game by starting with the end in mind. I recently worked on a lease of a 99,500-square-foot freestanding industrial building in the Inland Empire. The landlord and the prior tenant kept the property in such great condition that there was almost no friction or delay, causing the amount of work needed to prep the space for the new credit tenant to be minimal and the new tenant to move in seventeen days after the prior tenant moved out.

SURRENDER & RESTORATION
Similarly, a portion of the lease will be devoted to "surrender and restoration." Surrender dictates how the tenant returns the property to the landlord, whereas restoration refers to any tenant-specific improvements that need removal.

If, at the time of your existing tenant's lease signing, there was a large tenant improvement construction project, or if, at some point in time in their tenancy, the tenant expanded their tenant improvements (TI), you will want to review your restoration clauses within the lease document. The idea here is that the tenant needs to complete the demolition of specialized tenant improvements before the lease expiration date arrives.

We usually write the language so that you can choose whether you want to keep the specialized TIs or ask the tenant to remove them. Now is the time to see which existing tenant improvements add or detract from the property's leasability and to remove any detrimental tenant improvements at the tenant's sole cost and expense.

SECURITY DEPOSIT

The security deposit protects the landlord from the tenant not faithfully discharging their lease obligations. You now have your tenant's move-out condition language, walked the property, and decided what the tenant needs to remove and restore when surrendering the property possession back to you. Now is also the moment to understand your potential exposure in expenses compared to the security deposit on file.

Bob Andrews of Centerpoint Properties explains that the best practice is to "double-check the expiration date of your letter of credit. Imagine if your tenant was in holdover for a few months while they transitioned properties, and the letter of credit expired. What if your tenant was in default by not returning the property to you in the proper condition, and there was no valid letter of credit standing? Protect yourself from that."

Double-checking the letter of credit may not relieve the tenant of their ultimate responsibility to honor the contract, and you should still be able to enforce the lease in court. But that would necessitate the time and effort of initiating a lawsuit, and if you were successful in your lawsuit, you would still have to collect the judgment and self-fund the property restoration while waiting for the funds. Even if this scenario is unlikely, this is financial and legal exposure that is easily avoided by verifying and validating your letters of credit.

What if the amount of work that is needed exceeds the security deposit? What if the tenant that is moving out is doing so because of financial difficulties? Tenants who are bad actors may try to game the security deposit return process by not paying rent the last month of the lease, hoping the landlord won't take them to court to recoup any security deposit shortfall. It is always best to be up front when protecting your interests and enforcing the lease contract concerning the security deposit.

KEY TAKEAWAYS

- Think through when the optimal time is to reach out to your tenant to discuss renewing based on market conditions.
- Stay close to your existing tenant so you know what their true needs are in advance.
- Try your best to really understand your tenant's primary business drivers and operational use of the property so you can get a sense for its value to their overall enterprise.
- Know that tenants may act like they are moving in order to create leverage.
- Be clear on your move-out conditions.
- Set up a walk through to help gauge your tenants' true intentions.
- Communicate your property condition expectations after inspecting the property.
- Be mindful of what tenant-specific TIs you want restored.
- Understand the relation between the amount of security deposit on file and the cost to restore the property to first-class condition.

NEXT STEPS

Now that we have counseled you about how to deal with your impending lease expiration, it is time to think through who you will work with to find the next tenant that will add value to your property to maximize its ability to generate cash flow. We'll cover that in the next chapter that focuses on broker selection.

CHAPTER 5

BROKER SELECTION

MARKET ENGAGEMENT IS ONE OF THE MOST FUN PARTS of the process for leasing brokers: the positioning of the property, the crafting of the strategy, the proving of one's credentials, the big moment of introducing the property to the marketplace, and the hunt to lock in the best deal possible.

Perhaps the most important thing you can do regarding market engagement is select the right broker, as they are your spokesperson in the marketplace. They are your fiduciary, and their interaction will directly reflect on you as an owner and how your property will be received by brokers, tenants, and vendors alike.

One multi-tenant industrial business park in Lake Forest, California, consists of 100,000 square feet and was owned by an institutional investor with a larger portfolio of properties across the country. They were learning that owning, managing, and leasing multi-tenant properties in house was difficult to do profitably and that outsourcing their leasing was in their best interest.

When it came time to think and talk about whom to select to be their leasing brokerage team, they had an internal discussion about who was young and hungry in the business that might be a good fit for a project that consisted of fifty small tenants and ten medium-sized tenants, which would require extra effort to lease effectively. They decided that the best person for the project would be someone they already knew and trusted and had worked with in the past. There was no better broker than the broker who had recently brought them several tenants and knew the specific leasing process of this landlord.

This would turn out to be how our team received the majority of our leasing assignments, by being a hardworking, trustworthy team that was active in the market, trying to add value to every interaction with people.

BROKER SELECTION

Brokers have the opportunity to bring you the off-market acquisition opportunities that you desire. They are the people who will ultimately bring you your new tenant for your property. They are also the ones who will help you sell your fully leased building to attain the profit you envisioned when you first bought your property. Find a broker who has the kind of energy that you are looking for, and who has the skills that best fit your project.

Almost all institutional investors will tell you that the brokerage industry is the lifeblood of industrial real estate. They rely on brokers to be the boots on the ground and the finger on the pulse of the marketplace. One asset manager client of ours has acquired, invested, and managed $30 billion of real estate for hundreds of US and non-US institutional investors. He explains that they "have rotating meetings with brokers for roundtable discussions to understand where the market is heading. This critical input helps us solidify our game plan and process for the coming year with our asset management, property management, leasing, and portfolio management teams."

In any transaction, there is a landlord broker and a tenant broker who represent their respective parties at the negotiating table. One institutional asset manager who manages millions of square feet across the United States explains, "Brokers provide their clients with insights about their experiences dealing with different landlords and can have a material impact on who ultimately gets the deal. We are very broker friendly. Brokers source deals for us on the acquisitions side, whether it be land, off the market, or a fully marketed deal, no matter the source of the acquisition. Brokers represent the vast majority of credit tenants. I can't think of anyone of credit recently that didn't have a broker. We love having brokers on our listings because they have the best pulse of the market. Brokers have the true inside track to where deals are going down and understand the nuances of every deal. They know the intricacies of the comps and crucial deal points."

Regarding lease renewals, your protocol needs to be more uniform. Some landlords will try to represent themselves in lease renewals if they do not have an acquisitions broker associated with their property. Other landlords will have a broker in all lease renewals based on their fiduciary responsibility to their investors. And yet many landlords will opportunistically try to engage with the tenant directly independent of their broker and their tenant's broker. Landlords who try to keep brokers out of a transaction often do so in order to forgo paying broker commissions.

Investors who take this tact often bring in their broker if the tenant decides to bring in their broker to level the playing field. One challenge with this no-broker approach is during tumultuous economic cycles. During these times, there is a greater need to understand and educate the market. During the last three years, there have been countless issues between landlords and tenants as rental rates doubled and tripled, leading to stand-offs, impasses, erratic behavior, holdover, move-out, and more unnecessary friction. Half of this friction could have been avoided by having two professionals in the middle to educate and create a buffer space for candid conversations and deal-making.

Additionally, when you start without a broker, then you insert one midway, you can run into misalignment of incentives. When a landlord attempts to forgo paying brokerage commissions and keep the tenant from being represented, it can lead to a pause in relations. If the tenant comes back to the negotiating table deciding that they need representation and the landlord refuses to pay a tenant broker, then the tenant broker will be incentivized to move the tenant to a new building. This is not right or wrong—it is just a challenge that is created that can sometimes be self-defeating.

As a landlord you are balancing your property P&L, and saving on commission can improve your property P&L, but if you are so rigid that you lose tenants because of ostracizing their broker, then you may face downside risk by losing a tenant, having vacancy, and having to re-tenant the building, which will include new tenant improvements, and then ending up paying a new tenant leasing commission that is often at a rate higher than a standard lease renewal commission rate.

Institutional investors like Link Logistics have a sizable portfolio across the county. Emma Miller with Link Logistics explains, "We place a large emphasis on reporting and analyzing market dynamics to inform our decision-making. Much of that information comes from weekly conversations with my brokers. Brokers live in the deal-making process and represent other institutional investors and tenants in the marketplace. That makes them an important source of truth about what is happening at any given moment. We can then share this intelligence with our regional teams to provide them with a holistic view of the marketplace. By investing in our relationships with brokers and coupling that with our proprietary research and data analysis capabilities, we can stay ahead of the curve and continue to drive market opportunities."

PROTECTING RELATIONSHIPS

The most common strategy to implement when choosing your leasing broker is to return to the broker you worked with when you bought the building. This is the honor code in the commercial real estate industry.

Suppose the broker who helped the owner acquire the property has maintained positive working relationships. In that case, there is an expectation that the owner will work with that broker again when it comes time to lease the building. In that case, there is also the expectation that they will be hired again when the owner chooses to sell the property. Great brokers aspire to work with their clients for life and help them with anything they need.

Hayes Graham, Vice President of Acquisitions and Asset Management in Terreno Realty's San Francisco office, explains that "it comes down to looking at past deals, relationships, interactions, and how that broker has maintained his position within the community. We ask around to see how that broker is perceived by their peers. We think through how the broker personality works within our internal team. You have to have open and honest conversations and two-way communication. You must ensure the broker will do a great job presenting us and our interests."

Within that dynamic, though, things happen, right? Change is natural. People are hired, fired, or promoted. They retire, move across the country, start their own companies, and change careers. Such changes can impact your relationship with your broker. In cases where your broker is no longer available or is not getting the job done, you need a process for picking the right person for the job and establishing a relationship with them.

DeVonne Boler points out, "When we have to select brokerage firms for assignments that did not already have a broker assigned to them, we spread the assignments around the brokerage community so that no one brokerage controls all of the property, and so that we can maintain great relationships among all the brokerage firms that we rely on for tenants and new acquisitions."

Another consideration, in specific cases, is when your existing tenant has their space on the market for sublease. John Quinn of First Industrial explains, "I will sometimes consider working with the same broker for his property if I don't already have an existing relationship on that asset, as it can be beneficial to have a broker who is already familiar with the existing tenant's use and the property. Sometimes, having the tenant broker representing the sublease also represent us as a landlord, leads us to find a way to renew the tenant. Either way, it gives us a jump start on the assignment and finding the right-fit tenant."

SOURCING

The first step in finding the right broker is to ask your close network about brokers they know, like, and trust. Accountants and attorneys are great people to ask because they work with brokers frequently and often have inside information about the broker's relative quality and expertise. Additionally, brokers can contact your accountant when buying or selling an investment property to ensure the property is congruent with your tax and estate plan. The same goes for your attorney.

Next up is to see who is active in the market. If you drive around in your local market, look for whose names appear on the leasing and for-sale signs on the various buildings. Keep track of the phone calls, emails, mailings, and postcards you get from brokers soliciting you as a client.

Brokers are shameless self-promoters who use these outbound efforts to source relationships. Reach out to a few of them to begin a relationship and see if any might fit what you are looking for.

When it comes to institutional investors, there is rarely a formal presentation. Most often, there are already relationships between the landlord and brokerage community, and landlords can tap people whom they feel would be a good fit.

EVALUATION

The epitome of a broker you do *not* want is one who puts up a sign and waits for the phone to ring. You want someone hungry for the project and with a real tenacity for success.

For starters, you want to look for how well your broker knows the data that is driving the market, their team, track record, specialization, and marketing prowess. References are always welcome, too. This is where a broker can shine by demonstrating their ability to walk a mile in your shoes as an investor.

MARKET DATA / DATA ANALYSIS

Jack Cline, President of Lee & Associates' downtown Los Angeles office, explains, "Clients need to know that they can rely on the broker's information. The broker must give clients a clear understanding of the marketplace. This is a large component of what allows clients to make the best decision possible."

Knowing your market doesn't trump being a good broker with a track record of success and a great marketing machine, but it is most invaluable. Being a master of market data goes a long way because you don't want to take what the market will give you. You want to make the market. Making the market means knowing the property's intrinsic value to the market participants and maximizing that value.

Questions to ask about recently leased property ("lease comps"):

- What similar property was recently leased nearby?
- What conditions caused those lease terms to be achieved?
- What does that mean for my property?

Questions to ask about current property available for lease:

- What property is currently available that is directly comparable?
- How is that property being received by the market?
- What does that mean for my property?

Questions to ask about leasing trends:

- How has the demand and supply for similar properties changed this year?
- What is the sentiment in the marketplace right now?
- What are tenants looking for?

Regarding lease comp data, your broker should cross-reference and verify. And the larger the assignment, the more imperative that your broker has a team member to source, standardize, and synthesize lease data to forecast and infer where the market is heading.

TRACK RECORD

A track record of success is important. It does not have to mean that they have done the exact assignment one hundred times before (although that can be great). No two assignments are identical because of the unique nature of the property markets. Prior success means that the broker has built a habit of taking ownership of the success of projects and can communicate that.

Jack Cline of Lee & Associates' downtown Los Angeles office reminds us, "There is no reason you can't treat both sides fairly. There is no need for brokers to take an adversarial approach. You can do what is right and what is in the client's best interest and guide them with your experience, information, and judgment by being straightforward and truthful. Not only that, but if I'm doing my job right, I'm not only putting my client first, but I've given them options so that they have more than one choice. This allows clients to match up with business opportunities that align with their values and culture."

SPECIALIZATION

Specialization can be a differentiator in some cases. Areas of specialization for brokers include these:

- Practice Segment: Landlord vs. tenant vs. investment sale
- Property Type: Big box vs. shallow bay, industrial outdoor storage properties, cold storage, food production, life science, etc.
- Geographic: Submarket, city, county, and trade area

The more specialized the property you have to lease, the more important having a broker team with a specialization will be. You are looking for the alignment of market knowledge, skills, interests, and enthusiasm here.

MARKETING PROWESS

Your broker's marketing prowess will determine who is aware of your property and how it is perceived by the marketplace, and it will help tenants understand how your property will match your prospective tenant's vision for the future and their operation. Keep your eyes open for how savvy your broker is in the marketing department by assessing the following traits: creative, pricing strategy, positioning, promotion, follow-up, nurturing, and open house.

REFERENCES

If you are on the fence in your decision on whom to work with, ask for references, and call them. The commercial real estate community is a small and tight-knit community. It won't take more than a few calls to get a very good feel for that broker's standard operating procedure and reputation.

TEAMWORK

Great brokers don't always have a large team or formalized team, but increasingly the best do. There is simply too much work to develop, win, and execute at a high level for one person alone.

Most landlords prefer working with teams. Second, a team is usually made up of complementary strengths. In Rod Santomassimo's *Commercial Teams Built to Dominate,* Rod reviews several different team structures. Most powerhouse teams have a variety of senior brokers, junior brokers, and support staff. The benefit here is that you can leverage the wisdom and judgment of the senior broker, the energy and hustle of the junior broker, and the organizational skills of the support staff. When done right, the workflow feels effortless as each player knows their role in each assignment.

DeVonne Boler of Prologis echoes what many top-leasing managers and asset managers express: "We prefer to have a team on all of our listings. It allows us to be more nimble, have someone present for each tour and appointment, and cover for each other."

Don't just think of the brokerage team working for you when you think of teamwork. As Craig Viergiver, Executive Vice President and perennial top producer in Lee & Associates' Atlanta office, explains, "Our job is to make the asset manager's job as easy as possible. Too many brokers pass on the information and ask for a response. You must add value at every step and always have the next action step thought out, drafted, and in the asset manager's hands, ready for discussion and action. When you make that asset manager more efficient, informed, and powerful, guess what? You are going to get more business along the way by performing."

Jack Cline of Lee & Associates' Los Angeles office reminds us of the virtues of trust. "We are very sensitive to the idea that we have a cooperative reputation and operation. You must understand that it is a virtuous feedback loop between tenants, landlords, brokers, and cooperating brokers. That keeps people calling back and the wheels of commerce turning. This is something we work very hard to nurture."

PRICING STRATEGY

Pricing property for lease is both an art and a science. The science starts with the lease comps that establish the initial ballpark for pricing. The science continues with market leasing velocity and absorption to frame how the market is ascending, descending, or transitioning. Part of the art form, on the other hand, is having a feeling for how much to push rents, understanding a tenant's willingness to pay, or understanding how to balance vacancy and lower lease rates in a downturn.

Sometimes the pricing strategy is not to put a price on it. We often list properties without a price and put "withheld" or "to be determined." The most common time for this tactic is in a hot market where rates are in flux or demand is high. We don't want to advertise a price we'd have to stick to if prices increase. We want the flexibility to shift with the market and discover how much we can push.

The power of pricing flexibility is seen in a job where the landlord knew they needed eight months for renovation on their 47,000-square-foot building in the Inland Empire. At the start of the project, we had terminated a tenant's lease at $0.75 per square foot per month. Two weeks before the end of the renovation, the market was $1.40 per square foot per month, which is the price at which we closed the next lease contract. This is an extreme example during a once-in-a-lifetime ramp-up, but it was the quintessential use case for this strategy. If we had set a price, we would have had to change it repeatedly, which would have led to contradicting narratives in the marketplace.

Your pricing strategy can also be determined by the type of lease you prefer: triple net, modified gross, or gross. As a quick refresher, triple net leases exclude proportional fees for property tax, insurance, and maintenance fees, meaning that tenants pay those in addition to rent. In contrast, modified gross leases exclude property tax and insurance, and gross leases often don't exclude any additional expenses and are thought of as all-inclusive. Virtually all institutions utilize triple net leases for industrial property at present.

Usually, in a down cycle, landlords and their brokers offer concessions up front to attract a tenant with seemingly countless properties to move to. In down cycles, there are a handful of pricing schemes available, such as offering free rent, half rent, moving allowances, broker bonuses, and other leasing concessions.

POSITIONING

When it comes to positioning the property, it is all about creating an angle for your property. As Kevin Kelly, legendary Silicon Valley figure and longtime Wired executive who is author of the article "1,000 True Fans," explains, "You don't want to be the best—you want to be the only." Or if you take Peter Thiel's and Blake Masters's message in their book, *Zero to One*, the idea is that you want to create a position for your property within the marketplace that is undeniable to prospective tenants.

For example, you might be the only property with the unique combination of property attributes, in a given geographic area, at the attractive price, with that specific trade area locational advantage, and within a certain robust labor market, during a specific point in time. Ideally, your property will represent the only chance for a prospective tenant to be able to capitalize on a market opportunity for business growth using your property as leverage.

Great brokers think through how your property will fulfill the needs of the marketplace, and they craft a narrative that will permeate all parts of the marketing process to highlight your property's competitive advantage.

PROMOTION

In terms of promotion, your brokerage team should tell you the effective distribution channels where they will raise awareness for the property. Marketing campaigns should comprise inbound and outbound strategies to reach prospective tenants where they are. At a minimum, your broker should have a mastery of the following marketing channels:

- Canvassing the local trade area
- Outbound calls, emails, and mail to c-level executives, VPs of finance and operations, and general managers of best-fit prospects
- Economic development officers for states, counties, and cities based on the size and nature of the project
- Property-specific websites that are easily searchable and shareable
- Multiple listing services like CoStar, Loopnet, Crexi

- Social media presence via LinkedIn, Instagram, Facebook, Twitter
- Email newsletter directly to your broker's internal database of tenants, lenders, and vendors, architects, project managers, operations consultants, material handling and third-party logistics firms
- Property leasing sign or banner
- Professional networks for brokerage and property professionals like SIOR, NAIOP, CoreNet, IAMC
- Professional networks that are trade-related like CSCMPS, WERC, Cold Chain Alliance

Your team should actively go out and find your future tenant themselves. They should take ownership of the assignment and rely on their skills to produce the environment that will attract the tenant to your property. This is why investors have gravitated toward teams in the last decade, as most brokerage teams like ours have a senior broker, multiple associates, and additional marketing and support staff that all help assist. You must ensure that your property promotion efforts don't fall by the wayside because your team lacks the process or focus to follow through on marketing campaigns.

Outbound prospecting to tenants is not only promotion—it is intelligence. As DeVonne Boler points out, "We rely on our brokers to be the eyes and ears for us, to have their finger on the pulse of the brokerage community, and to help us have the best marketplace representation possible." When prospecting, brokers figure out who is growing, what challenges tenants are facing within the business climate, how they are weighing their decisions, and why they are selecting certain properties over others.

Craig Viergiver, Executive Vice President of Lee & Associates' Atlanta office, explains, "We help tenants understand the ownership structure of the landlords we work for. Tenants want to know that they are aligning with the right landlord."

And don't forget about how the actual tour is going to work. Jack Cline of Lee & Associates' downtown Los Angeles office explains, "We do our best to have someone at every tour. That is where the objections and issues are surfaced and best heard, understood, and addressed."

CREATIVE

Subpar marketing collateral is not acceptable. Brokers should select the appropriate creative for the project based on the needed photography, aerials, floor plans, site plans, property-specific websites, videography, drone photos, videos, Matterport 3D virtual tours, etc. The variety of investments between the individual and the brokerage firm is soup to nuts, from literally nothing to a $20,000 investment in a professionally outsourced marketing package. What is appropriate will be based upon who your target audience is and what works best to resonate with them.

Great firms elevate their marketing efforts by having in-house and third-party graphic design teams that will make sure the marketing materials adhere to their brokerage's brand standards. They will also look to provide accurate, clean, and easy-to-read floor plans, professional site plans, and an overall polished design that make the marketing materials attractive and memorable.

Help tenants visualize their pallet racking, truck loading, and office layout. Add renderings, racking layouts, floor plans, site plans, dimensions, hypothetical improvements, and anything that shows how one can maximize the use of the property when appropriate. Don't wait for tenants to engage their imagination. Give them examples. Make it easy for them. Executives prize speed to market.

FOLLOW UP

All veteran brokers will tell you that the money is in the follow-up. Once you have generated interest in your property, it's important to follow up with potential tenants and maintain communication.

Tenants and tenant brokers aren't always active on an assignment and ready to take action on your property when you initially reach them. Implementing a powerful Customer Relationship Management (CRM) System like Salesforce can help you manage and track all your interactions with potential tenants, ensuring that no leads slip through the cracks. This involves sending regular updates on property availability, sharing relevant news and insights about the local market, and addressing any questions or concerns they may have. This nurturing and follow-up will help keep your property top of mind and increase the likelihood of converting leads into tenants.

OPEN HOUSE

One way we attract tenants is by holding a broker open house. Commercial real estate open houses are not like residential open houses, which are more like office hours in that they are an opportunity to bring in neighbors and buyers directly to the property to learn more. These broker open houses are to raise awareness within the brokerage community, to control the narrative of how the property is presented, and then to gain valuable feedback from the brokerage community.

But the brokerage community is eternally busy and focused solely on what makes them commission as they are in an eat-what-you-kill, commission-only business. This is why a leasing broker needs to have a good relationship with the brokerage community and needs to have creativity to get a great turnout.

It's all about making it fun, hosting everyone, providing food and drink, providing giveaways, and then making sure that the brokers all know about the ownership, ownership's plan for the building, and why it stands out as an opportunity worth bringing clients to. Hosting can be as simple as a few round tables and folding chairs or the In-N-Out Burger truck. Open houses can include driving through the building, taking out golf carts and ATVs on a construction site, and riding scooters to get around the large warehouse area. Giveaways can include gift certificates, tickets to the Lakers' playoff game, or a six-pack of beer. You would be amazed how much influence an open house can have as it provides instant awareness and word of mouth within the brokerage community. Brokers who attend can now visualize the property when speaking with tenants in the market and sizing up opportunities.

REPORTING

While your broker is searching for a tenant, asking for periodic progress reports is more than reasonable. This way, you can rest assured that your broker did not simply stick a sign in the ground and wait for their phone to ring.

You want to give your broker the autonomy to execute the marketing campaign and to leverage their interpersonal skills, network, and team to the best of their ability. At the same time, great brokers will want to report their progress to clients to provide visibility and transparency regarding what is happening with the property. Regular reporting creates a strong working relationship and more importantly a two-way continuous feedback loop that makes for optimal decision-making.

Brokers have numerous ways to deliver these reports to you. Timely updates over the phone are the minimum standard. Many institutional leasing teams like ours utilize a leasing platform like VTS, which provides real-time visibility across all pertinent people within the investor and brokerage teams.

PROSPECT REPORT

The standard leasing prospect report details each tenant's name, tenant broker's name, the tenant's level of interest, the status of the lead's progress, and any other noteworthy details.

The feedback in the notes section is hugely beneficial to you. For example, prospects and their brokers may tell your broker that the space is overpriced. As the landlord, you want to know what the market is saying about your space so you can adjust if you are out of line or the market dynamic is changing. Prospective tenants will tell your broker if the building doesn't show well or if aspects of it are not functional for their business.

Perhaps most importantly, this report is good for knowing that your broker is staying engaged with tenants and tenant brokers, that the broker is overcoming objections and challenges, and that they are communicating effectively with you.

The frequency of this report may vary. Determine the appropriate frequency to give your broker autonomy but also cultivate visibility. Every two to four weeks is most common.

VTS, originally known as View the Space, specializes in providing a portal for property owners, asset managers, property managers, and investment committees, with access to real-time feedback from their brokers. Other startups and software options specialize in this, but VTS is the biggest player at the time of this writing.

VTS houses all your asset and lease data in one place, where your broker inputs the details of all leasing activity for that asset and the available building or space. This system eliminates the need to look through your overcrowded email of thousands of undeleted spam for relevant updates from your broker. Instead, VTS will house everything pertinent to leasing your building in one place. It includes your building rent roll and pertinent prospective tenant information, including tour feedback, letters of intent, and deal economics.

If you are the landlord of just one building or are reluctant to add another application to your tech stack, VTS might be overkill. And, in a hot market, you may not need to keep track of all your prospects because there's another one right around the corner. But this approach is worth considering if you have many properties with leases, multiple brokers to track, or layers of management that need real-time visibility.

One multibillion-dollar private equity fund asset manager describes how VTS helps his team, which is distributed across multiple offices around the country, have real-time access to information. "You can go from high-level, portfolio-wide analytics to drilling down on the individual asset level in seconds. Managing multiple assets helps me quickly retrieve rent roll analysis and budgets and assess exposure on the spot. This is especially helpful when you have multiple multi- and single-tenant industrial assets and have a high velocity of lease signings."

This resonates with efficiency consultant Nick Sonnenberg's book *Come Up for Air*, where he describes that the best businesses don't optimize for the speed of transmittal of information, but for the retrieval of information. VTS is one of those tools for institutional investors that will continue to grow in the commercial real estate investment business as it optimizes for the retrieval of all pertinent leasing information.

It boils down to visibility. As Craig Viergiver of Lee & Associates' Atlanta office puts it, "Not only does this help asset managers, but it helps equity partners drill down to the asset level as needed."

TENANTS IN THE MARKET

Tenants in the Market (TIM) is one of these reports that dovetails with the prospect report. Suppose the prospect report is a log of every prospect who has inquired into the property, whose broker has inquired into the property, or whom your brokers have dug up for your property. In that case, the Tenants in the Market report resembles an aggregate of multiple prospect reports.

Landlord listing teams with many listings will have more exposure to tenant requirements. Well-connected brokers continually network within the community of landlord listing brokers and hear who is working on what. Brokers who work with larger firms have regular meetings to discuss who is in the market. All of these information sources enhance tenant intelligence that allows you to understand what deals you are not seeing, the depth of the pool of prospects in the market, and the velocity of new requirements coming into the market. For example, your leasing team can get a sense of how many square feet of active lease requirements are in the market in relation to the number of square feet of property actively being marketed. If you knew that there were 10 million square feet of active requirements and only 3 million square feet of property available, you would take one tact with prospects. If that 10 million changes to 4 million because of economic headwinds, you would be able to shift approaches with tenants accordingly.

As a result, you may ask your team to reach out to one of the tenants that didn't inquire about your property. In a slow market, your broker can send them a lease proposal. This will also give you the sixth sense to know if you should take the deal in hand or punt and wait for the next opportunity.

COMPETITIVE SET

The competitive set report is one that very process-driven institutional landlords request quarterly or annually. This is a study that we produce showing all the competing projects. We then detail the project's ownership structure, vacancy rates, lease rate, leasing concessions, broker bonuses, TI packages, operating expenses, and notes about how they are perceived in the brokerage community.

Once my team and I integrated this into our practice, we found it a no-brainer to provide to all of our clients to give the context needed for investors to really understand the competitive landscape to make informed decisions.

Because there are so many different reporting options, it's good to ask your broker their opinions of reporting and see if they align with your feelings. Ask:

- What kind of reporting do you provide during the project?
- How often do you think it is appropriate to provide updates?
- What is your process for providing updates?

KEY TAKEAWAYS

- The honor code in the commercial real estate brokerage business allows the broker who sold you the project the ability to continue to lease and sell it provided they maintain the relationship and provide great service.
- When it is time to make a change, or to start from scratch, ask your professional network for recommendations.
- When evaluating brokers, understand their mastery of market data, team strength, track record, specialization, and marketing prowess.
- Ask brokers how they would approach pricing, positioning, and promotion of your property. Ask how their creativity will be used to attract tenants. Ask how they follow up with leads to nurture them until they are ready.
- Ask brokers how they handle reporting, tenants in the market, and competitive sets.
- When in doubt, call references to understand what level of service your prospective broker has provided other similar clients.

NEXT STEPS

Finding your perfect-fit broker is a moment to behold when all that was potential now seems possible. Now it is time for the rubber to meet the road in signing up your broker and getting on with the marketing campaign to attract the best tenant possible.

CHAPTER 6

LISTING AGREEMENTS

THE LISTING AGREEMENT IS THE FIRST CONTRACT YOU sign, leading up to the final lease contract. Most brokerages have standard forms.

During this phase, you can see the broker's closing skills. They will try and close you on why you should work with them. Seeing how they close you will foreshadow how they work with potential tenants. Within the framework of the contract, there are several details that are worth considering.

Our team regularly takes over listings from other brokerage firms that cannot deliver on a specific assignment. This can happen for a multitude of reasons from brokers having a mismatch of needed skills to having a key team member leave, or sometimes just because of a difficult negotiation experience.

When we take over listings from other teams, we often have to negotiate exclusions within a listing agreement. An exclusion is a way for the old broker to be protected on lease deals that they have pending during the transition of brokerage teams. On one 65,000-square-foot listing in Santa Ana, California, the landlord asked us to work with the old broker on an exclusion in our new listing agreement. The old broker had shown the property to a group that was talking about submitting a lease proposal but had not actively done so yet. This is a gray area in leasing that can sometimes be more subjective than objective.

The landlord trusted me to handle the matter as I saw fit. It was up to me to decide what the right course of action was to honor the landlord, my firm, my team, and the prior broker. In the end I decided that protecting the previous broker on that one exclusion was the right thing to do, and then I negotiated a fair amount of time for that protection and the stipulations that would cause that protection to expire in short order to allow us to move on with the assignment without further obstacles.

LENGTH OF TERM

Listing lengths have various sizes and terms, the standard being six months. There are several reasons, though, why you may deviate.

First, shorter listing agreements are not advisable. On odd occasions, high-net-worth landlords will think that keeping their broker "on a short leash" gives the broker the urgency to get the job done before they are fired. Occasionally younger brokers will accept this in hopes that they will be lucky and be able to complete the assignment in time or in hopes that they can negotiate a further extension of that listing agreement. It is usually a disservice to have an unreasonably short listing agreement as it disincentivizes the broker to invest time, effort, and resources into the project if the chances of a return on that investment don't seem likely.

Reasons for a more extended listing agreement are many. The main ones are if you have new construction, you have a large property repositioning construction project, you get an early notice that a tenant will move out, or you have a multi-tenant business park with numerous spaces that need leasing regularly.

The mechanism for renewing expired listing agreements is usually to have the broker provide a letter to the landlord for them to sign that extends the listing for six to twelve months. To save time on constantly renewing listing agreements on long-term listing assignments, some landlords will provide a listing term that "auto-renews" until there is a written termination to the contrary.

MASTER SERVICE AGREEMENT

Some institutional landlords will do enough work with firms to have a master service agreement with listing-specific addendums. The idea here is to have faster execution speeds by having predefined listing contract terms.

EXCLUSIONS

An exclusion is a contract carve out that can occur when a tenant is in active negotiation for a lease. Still, the landlord is firing and replacing their broker anyway. You might wonder why the landlord would fire a broker if they brought in a potential tenant. Sometimes this is because a broker is actually being fired. However, the likely instance is that the listing agreement expired, and the broker will not be rehired. Exclusions are like estoppels in that the purpose is to provide a clean slate from one party to the next. This might mean reengaging with the tenant that the fired broker targeted.

Exclusions could also occur when the property changes hands. Maybe the new owner works with their leasing firm, which differs from the seller's. When the property changes hands, exclusions will allow the next brokers to come in with a clean slate and start from scratch. Any lease negotiations would be dropped, so the tenants must work with the new brokers.

SCHEDULE OF COMMISSIONS

When finalizing the contract with the broker, you should receive a schedule of commissions. This document details who gets paid, how much they get paid, any caveats, and when everybody gets paid.

So who gets paid? That seems obvious, the listing broker. The tenant broker's commissions are also covered here, as the landlord pays both brokers. But the listing agreement and schedule of commissions is an agreement between the landlord and the landlord broker. There is no tenant broker at the time of signing. As a result, you will often see tenant brokers of more significant transactions or tenant-rep-only firms ask for a commission agreement to be signed between them and the landlord once they have agreed to terms on a deal. You may also see tenant brokers ask for a commission amount different from what you signed up for in your listing agreement with your broker. The common tenant broker retort is, "I don't let landlord brokers negotiate my fee." It's not wrong per se to have a tenant broker ask for a different amount. It just depends on why and how much.

A typical example is the landlord broker's need to request a lower total commission amount to get the assignment. Then the tenant broker comes in with a tenant that has choices. When other landlords are happy to pay a market commission compared to a landlord offering a lesser tenant broker commission, the tenant broker will often ask to be paid whatever is commonplace in the market.

What if the tenant doesn't have a broker? This doesn't happen very often on sizable deals, but it does on small multi-tenant projects all the time. How much does your broker get paid when there is no tenant broker? Does it matter if your broker also represents the tenant? These are questions you'll want to have answers to or ask your broker about.

What about renewals? Most institutional landlords will work renewals on their own and only call brokers into the negotiation table if their tenant engages their broker. Some older leases state that the tenant's broker will be paid on all renewals and expansions at the time of renewal.

The amount of money the brokers make can substantially change depending on the state, municipality, and geography of the deal. It can change based on the state of the market as well. It will also vary based on the size of the project and whether the project is in its initial lease-up phase. It can also depend on whether the commission is based on the total net, gross, or modified gross rent schedule. It will depend on the role of the broker, whether landlord or tenant. The most commonly used industrial leasing commission schedule is 6 percent of the total consideration, and it can be as low as 4 percent to as high as 7.5 percent for the leasing agent. For the tenant broker, it could be anywhere from 2.5 percent to 5 percent, with the remaining balance going to the landlord's agent.

While it is possible to try to grind down your broker's leasing schedule, I have found it rarely achieves the landlord's objective, finding a quality creditworthy tenant at the highest rate, with the least concessions, with little to no vacancy, to maximize the value of their industrial real estate. If you disincentivize your broker, you will lessen their respect for the assignment. If you disincentivize the tenant or broker, they will be more motivated to take their tenant's business elsewhere. As one of my favorite clients whom I've worked with across the nation in ten states over the last ten years says, "There is no reason why we can't compensate everyone fairly."

DUAL AGENCY

Dual agency is when the same firm, and sometimes the same broker or brokerage team, represents both the landlord and the tenant. In these situations, a single percentage point discount to the commission is normal if the same brokerage firm or team represents both parties. The idea is that the landlord broker can do the same amount of work in less time than if two brokers were involved so that savings can be passed to the landlord while the broker is still compensated more than if there were a tenant broker. This last part is crucial because it can further motivate your landlord broker to continue to go out and find tenants and not rely on the tenant broker community.

One broker represents the landlord and tenant in a dual-agency situation. In some states, this is illegal either to have the same person or the same company representing both parties. The general thought process here is that the negotiation is zero-sum, and it is unethical to have one person who has a contract with the landlord to represent the landlord and represent the tenant. The typical example here is that of a legal trial where there is an attorney for either party in a civil trial or there is a prosecuting and defense attorney for a criminal trial. It is unthinkable to contemplate having one attorney represent the state and the person accused of a crime.

In the states where it is legal, there are protocols for one broker to demonstrate fiduciary responsibility to the two opposing parties. The duty or standard of care is elevated and more closely monitored during this situation. Ask any broker who operates in a state where dual agency is allowed, and they will tell you that it is more difficult to represent both parties simultaneously.

As you might imagine, dual agency can be fraught with opportunities for mismanagement. For instance, inexperienced brokers tasked with a dual-agency job may need to learn how to simultaneously protect the fiduciary interests of both parties, which can lead to legal issues.

If you are faced with a dual-agency situation and are concerned about conflicts of interest, you can approach your broker honestly to get answers to the following questions.

- How would you go about representing me fairly?
- What would be a challenge for you if you represented both sides?

Brokers who will succeed for both parties in dual-agency situations will 1) be very active and knowledgeable in the marketplace in such a manner that will attract multiple tenants to generate competition for the landlord and 2) dwell on marketplace knowledge instead of personal knowledge when dealing with both parties to make prices fair.

PAYMENT

The timing of the commission will be essential to you. The standard operating procedure is that half of the leasing commission is due when the lease is fully executed, and the landlord receives all monies due. The second half of the commission is due when the tenant takes possession of the property. This taking possession of the property is only after the landlord receives the tenant's certificate of insurance that names the landlord as additionally insured.

There are exceptions to this rule. The main one has to do with when a soft market or a desirable tenant is being considered. In that instance, it can be commonplace for the tenant broker to request that brokerage commissions be paid when the lease is fully executed, and all monies are due.

The second exception is when there is a lease renewal. Many times landlord and tenant brokers negotiate on a lease that is set to expire in the next six to twelve months. Some landlords will want to change the timing of the payment of the leasing commission to half upon signing and half upon commencement.

Most landlords will pay within thirty days of lease signing because any delay in paying the second half of commissions conceptually is about the tenant taking possession of the property. In a lease renewal, the tenant is already in possession of the property. If you choose to delay paying the second half of the lease commission until after the renewal term starts, you will receive more cash flow before paying the second half of the commission. You will also irritate your broker and your tenant's broker who have been working for free up until the point of lease signing.

Brokers' expectations are to be paid for the value that is created, when it is created. For example, if a new lease extension is negotiated that increases the lease rate substantially, the landlord can immediately take the property to market with that lease extension in place and ask for a higher price based on the contract value of the new lease agreement, even though the lease extension isn't yet in effect. In this example you are already rewarded for having done the lease extension, and it creates goodwill to pay commissions at that time.

- Listing Agreement: Establish an appropriate contract length, consider exclusions, and negotiate commissions for a mutually beneficial relationship with the broker.
- Length of Term: Choose a term that supports the broker's efforts and the property's unique leasing needs.
- Master Service Agreement: Streamline the leasing process for frequent partnerships through predefined contract terms.
- Exclusions: Provide a clean slate for new brokers when the property changes hands or when replacing a broker during active tenant negotiations.
- Schedule of Commissions: Ensure fair compensation for all parties involved, considering various factors such as market conditions and deal size.
- Dual Agency: Exercise caution in dual-agency situations and ensure the broker can fairly represent both parties.
- Payment: Determine the appropriate timing for commission payments, considering market conditions, lease renewals, and tenant occupancy.

NEXT STEPS

This stage is one of the most exciting points in industrial real estate because it's time to take your well-crafted plan and release it into the world. This is when you start getting feedback from real prospects—from the check writers, as Dan Sullivan would say. What is the feedback from those who will write the check and sign the lease for leasing your building? Get to them, get them into the building, and get them thinking about how they can grow and prosper in your facility.

CHAPTER 7

TENANT SELECTION

ONCE YOU HAVE HIRED YOUR ALL-STAR TEAM OF BRO-kers and set them loose in the market in search of your ideal tenant, their job as listing brokers is to represent you in the marketplace and exchange market intelligence and property information.

We are in the match-making business at this point. Depending on the situation, we must be attentive, feign interest, be extra responsive, or act aloof. Our ultimate job is to get the tenant's executive to the property. Once there, we can shine and be empathetic and, as Joe Polish adeptly titled his latest book, focus on *What's in It for Them?* After that, we coach tenant brokers on how they can put their best foot forward in crafting a win-win lease proposal.

We have dozens of high-net-worth families who own industrial property and are looking for us to take charge and own the whole leasing process life cycle. This can include determining when and how to go to market, finding a property manager, deciding on what improvements to make, selecting an architect and general contractor, and more.

One illustrative project we worked on was a 50,000-square-foot industrial property in Santa Fe Springs, California. This was owned by the long-standing family who had built a successful business and purchased the property decades prior. After a change in ownership of the business, and a passing down of the property to the next generation, it was time for the whole business to move out of state and consolidate operations and for the family to carry on leasing the property.

Having modest experience, they were looking for a team they could lean on to walk them through every single step of the process. Here we had a functional property but one that had not been renovated in more than twenty years.

The trick here that moved mountains for this family was finding a credit tenant with a construction background that would perform their own tenant improvements in exchange for a free-rent equivalent. We did this all while preserving our negotiating leverage while bringing in multiple qualified tenants. In the end we wound up striking a long-term lease with a billion-dollar company that handles 95 percent of their own improvements. Not only did this shift the time and effort from the landlord to the tenant, but it wound up shifting the eventual construction pricing overrun risk onto the tenant as well.

PROPERTY TOURS

Imagine the ideal property tour. Elon Musk steps out of his broker's Mercedes Benz Sprinter van. The broker escorts him and his VP of operations across a newly slurried parking lot. They step over freshly painted parking stalls as they head toward the ADA-compliant walkway. The tenant executive team then walks through the propped-open double-glass door entry into the spec lobby where the lights are on and bright, where your brokerage team greets them alongside a three-by-four-foot leasing sign showing the property features and floor plans and a reception-area backsplash ready for company branding.

The collaborative teams walk through each part of the well-lit and ready-for-inspection building. Ultimately, the tenant's executive team walks into the warehouse to privately discuss how the property can fit their vision. They then meet with the landlord leasing team, answer questions, overcome objections, and present potential solutions. A solid rapport is built. Everyone leaves feeling deal potential in the air and agrees to have "our people talk with your people to sort out the details."

Now, with that as the gold standard, let's look at possible sources of friction that could get in the way so that we can elevate the experience beyond expectations.

PREPARATION

Great brokers on the property tour know to be early and prepared. The property and building should be as open as possible, with the lights on and a few dock doors open. The team should be well dressed, with presentation materials and a positive can-do attitude.

The first place inexperienced brokers fumble is with access to the space because it is either occupied or requires notice from the current tenant, which is done hastily. Or the property is vacant, the lockbox key is missing, the lockbox is rusted shut from the sprinklers, the combination doesn't work, or the lock doesn't open without toil. The prospect starts with a negative first impression when things like this happen. Few things start an interaction worse than this.

Once inside, prospects should be able to see what they're doing, so leave the power on to the building. Dark warehouses and office buildings look like creepy sets from a horror movie, filled with cobwebs and your garden-variety pests.

It is just as important for you to keep the water on. While walking a tenant in a restroom full of toilets and empty urinals with brown rings around the bottom is unsightly, if you don't keep the water on, you leave the impression that you don't have a restroom for a prospective tenant to use in case it is needed.

These things might seem like no-brainers, but if you are a less-experienced or ultra-frugal landlord transitioning into the new building owner, the transfer of utilities could cause issues where power and water are temporarily shut off. So, make sure you have that transition of utilities set up for the day of closing, and maintain and service the restrooms so check writers have a great experience at the property.

SECURITY

Security needs never stop. When you have a vacant property, people within the community will notice no cars showing up to the building anymore and no lights illuminating the interior, entryway, or parking lot. The people who realize this are neighboring businesses, their visitors, vendors, and anyone who happens to be in the area. Word gets out.

These vacant buildings can become prime targets for vandalization and theft. Vandals often break into buildings, turn the power off, cut all the conduit and copper lines, and drive off with them. They'll also remove all transfer switches, breaker panels, and anything electricity-related that has scrap value. You may be surprised that this theft is often not covered by insurance and can cost hundreds of thousands of dollars. Not only is the cost in dollars great, but the time that it takes for the local or regional electricity provider to bring service back to the property can take months, and oftentimes over a year.

With that in mind, put an alarm on your property. Buildings are broken into frequently. Brokers forget to return lockbox keys or lose them, or the lockbox is broken or even vandalized. Some vandals will even cut or drill the lockbox to get the key out to gain entry to the property.

For a nominal up-front and monthly spend, you can have a system that will notify you if a problem is brewing at your property. If you are reading this, and you own property for lease that is vacant, stop what you are doing, and consider arming your building now. Just do your future self a favor.

Alarms aren't perfect, of course. There are false alarms and snafus. Every broker with years in the business has been involved with or heard about a story where a property tour triggered the alarm and nobody could successfully disarm the system. The police showed up with guns drawn, thinking they were arriving at an armed robbery, just to find everyone embarrassingly standing there talking about how to lease the property. It can be awkward, but it's better to have that happen than to have your broker and prospective tenant show up to a building that is robbed of all of its copper and that *is* a crime scene.

If you own several available properties in a market, consider hiring a security patrol service to drive by your buildings each night. We did this with a favorite institutional investor in the Inland Empire. We were relieved that there was security to go by and double-check whenever something was amiss at the property. What you are looking for is a foolproof system of accountability. With an alarm, if it is going off or not armed, you can check on that and do something about it. Without an alarm, if some property element is vulnerable to theft, it can be hard to identify that problem and who is responsible for it.

You should have the security conversation up front with your brokers so that all parties have security, protocols, and goals in mind to minimize the risk as much as possible.

FEEDBACK

Once a tenant and tenant broker get through the property without friction, the main objective of your broker is to listen. Listen for feedback. Listen to what works. Listen to what doesn't. This will help establish whether the prospective tenant and the building match. The broker should also ask poignant and probing questions to discern whether the feedback sentiments are false or real objections. A great broker will encounter real objections and turn them into creative solutions.

During the tour, each component piece of the building will be examined regarding how it will work well with the prospective tenant. For an office-heavy industrial building, the broker might ask the tenant how many departments the company has, how many people there are, the preferred office size, and other questions that will help the broker gauge how to create an office space that works for the tenant. For the warehouse section of the building, the broker might ask how the company usually lays out its racking and what kind of product it's storing. For manufacturing operations, it is essential to consider what types of machines are being used, the process flow, and the power requirements for starters.

With feedback, you can adjust your general leasing approach and be specific to each tenant. Most importantly, you can be in a position to respond best to your ideal tenant's forthcoming letter of intent.

SPACE PLANNING

If you own an industrial property with a 10 percent or greater office component, your future will likely coincide with a general contractor's soon, as every tenant has their future layout in mind. Usually, there will be a second tour with the person signing the lease and sometimes with a space planner and architect. There, parties can get more detailed in how the tenant wants to use the space and about what construction, if any, must take place to meet those needs.

Who hires the space planner may vary. Office-building landlords likely have a space planner on retainer. In that situation, you may decide to bring your planner in. This cost may fall to the tenants if it's a smaller building or a low-volume owner. Some tenants lease so many spaces that they also might have their regular space planner that they bring on board. It just depends on the situation and specific circumstances.

This tour isn't going to be producing a final plan. The parties are doing their test fitting to see if the space will work when all the details are considered.

LOIS AND PROPOSALS

The first step *after* an interested party makes themselves known is receiving a lease proposal from the prospective tenant. It's pretty simple, and this part of the process has just a few mechanics. The proposal is usually called the letter of intent (LOI). Both will act as synonyms throughout the rest of the chapter.

REQUEST FOR PROPOSALS

When tenants want to look at multiple buildings, they may ask you for a request for proposal (RFP). This is a negotiation-strategy maneuver on the part of the tenant that will put you on the defensive in an attempt to offer discounts and concessions at the start of the negotiation process. The presumption of the tenant looking at multiple properties implies that *they*, and not the space, are the sought-after commodity.

This approach is usually seen with creditworthy tenants. They may send three to five RFPs to different landlords asking for competitive rates, tenant improvement packages, concessions, and other items you as the landlord will consider to induce them to continue negotiating with you.

I always advise clients to respond to RFPs. However, how we respond depends on the creditworthiness of the tenant, the market cycle, and the landlord's objectives. The big difference here is figuring out the tenant's operational needs, knowing your lease comps cold, and then making sure you hit at least one of the tenant's hot buttons in your response.

The best operational fit is usually the property the tenant wants to prioritize. Knowing how your property stacks up with competing properties will help you understand whether that is likely to be your property or whether it is another. This is where having a knowledgeable broker will help you make those estimates and factor them into the response.

LETTERS OF INTENT

If the tenant likes the space, they'll create an LOI and submit it to you. These letters register intent; they suggest the most basic lease terms the tenant prefers and open the negotiating process. There is an overt or implied need for you, the landlord, to reply to this letter and respond with the terms that work for you. Conversely, to the request for proposal, the letter of intent gives you the negotiation advantage. These letters will go back and forth until both parties have the same terms.

Another element determining the negotiation advantage is whether or not you are operating in a landlord or tenant market. When fewer spaces are available to tenants, the laws of supply and demand create a need for your space; that's a landlord market. You have your pick of tenants, and the plethora of options puts pressure on the tenant to meet your preferred terms. If the opposite is true—there are very few tenants and many empty spaces—you are in a tenant market. In a tenant market, you will sacrifice your desired lease terms to attract a limited number of tenants.

LOI TERMS

The LOI determines whether the two parties have enough common ground to strike a deal before spending legal fees and executives' time hammering out the details. About 80 percent of LOIs have the same categories. Some overly eager or corporate tenants will detail twenty to thirty lease terms within the LOI. In practice, this is rarely to anyone's benefit other than their ego.

And remember, don't start drafting a lease until you have an LOI that is 100 percent agreed to by both parties. Nothing wastes more time and goodwill than having an LOI that is mostly agreed to, where people assure the other party that they can figure the rest out in the lease negotiation, only to find that business terms are now being negotiated against legal terms. This frustrates everyone and rarely results in a positive outcome for both parties. Reasonable attorneys know this and usually won't start drafting a lease until they see both parties' signatures on the LOI.

As a landlord, you will be receiving tenant lease proposals. Upon reviewing them, you will want to read between the lines of what information is provided, what is missing, and what needs further clarification to address all deal terms adequately. Here are the terms you need to address up front:

USE

How will the tenant use the space? This could include storage, manufacturing, fulfillment and distribution, chemical processes, or a combination. As the landlord, knowing this information means you are aware of the potential impacts of the tenant's presence, including hazardous materials coming onto the property, noise pollution, or excessive use (and subsequent damage you'll have to fix later).

Further, determining use should lead to important and specific questions for the tenant. How many machines will they operate? What chemicals do they use? What kind of trucks will be on-site? Will the yard be used for storage? Follow-up questions will drive informed decisions and help you properly weigh risk versus reward.

Use questions will also help to give you a feel for whether any concerns are related to whether the tenant's use is allowed with the municipality's zoning matrix.

ENTITIES

These are the legal entities on the lease. Be firm about knowing what entity you will have on your lease contract. Are you getting General Motors, one of its subsidiaries, or a smaller outfit with a contract with General Motors?

DATES

There can be different critical dates. One is the commencement date, or when the tenant begins to pay rent. Another is the early occupancy date, when the tenant begins using specific parts (but not all) of the building, such as offices or warehouses, before the commencement of rent.

You may have situations where tenants want to move in, pay rent, and use part of the building before construction is complete. Further, these dates will likely change throughout the negotiation process, especially to accommodate changes to the construction schedule. So, having these dates understood helps clarify the needs.

TERM

This is where WALT comes into play. The weighted average lease term is the average lease term remaining in an industrial real estate portfolio or multi-tenant industrial asset when the asset is being sold. Why is WALT so important? WALT represents the length of commitments in place and the time until the next opportunity to create new lease value. By being mindful of any lease you are negotiating and its relationship to the property's sale value, you can ensure that the property value is being maximized for refinance, recapitalization, sale, or book value.

The term is the total amount of years the tenant agrees to occupy the space. The phrase "firm term" is the total years the tenant is locked into that space, not including renewals. For example, some may ask for a five-year lease with a five-year option to extend instead of a ten-year lease. They are not the same.

The lease term is usually five years for buildings sized 5,000 to 50,000 square feet. Anything above that can see lease terms of around ten, fifteen, and even twenty years.

BASE RATE

The base rate is the amount of monthly rent. This does not include operating expenses unless you are talking about a gross lease. It is fine to quote a PSF price here.

LEASE TYPE

The three standard leases are triple net, modified gross, or gross.

ANNUAL INCREASES

These are the increases in rent over the lease term. Utilizing the consumer price index (CPI) can determine the letter of intent's annual increase. At the time of writing, market hovers around 3 or 5 percent. It's variable and is often beholden to the market.

OPERATING EXPENSES

These are additional payments incurred by the tenant based on costs such as property tax, insurance, and maintenance. You can often estimate these amounts by looking at the property's performance in previous years in these areas. The three categories at play throughout CAMs are maintenance, repair, and replacement.

FREE RENT

The concept of free rent may seem obvious, but the structure is not. How many total months of rent are being offered, and when do these free months occur? The quantity and timing of free rent are market-cycle specific. I've worked on deals with zero free rent, and I've worked on deals with twelve months of free rent. You want to minimize, delay, be reimbursed if the tenant defaults, and set an expiration date for unused free rent. You also want to be clear that free rent is not free operating expenses. On a triple net (NNN) lease, that means all operating expenses. On a modified gross or gross lease, that may mean the CAMs and trash. It never means utilities.

Let's say you give two months of free rent on a 100,000-square-foot space that charges $2.00 per square foot NNN monthly ($24.00 per square foot NNN annually). Is it better to give those two months up front? Here are a few items to consider:

- How does this free rent affect your cash flow?
- How does this free rent affect your debt service?
- How much does the rent increase in subsequent years if there is free rent?
- How likely is it that the tenant will stay through each lease year?

TENANT IMPROVEMENTS

Informally referred to as TIs, these determine what the tenant needs to do to the building. TIs are the common source of friction in projects that are not fully renovated and with amateur landlords and tenants. The important questions to be included in this part of the negotiation are, Who will do the work, who is paying for it, and what happens if it is delayed or costs more?

Hayes Graham of Terreno echoes what many asset managers have experienced: "Credit isn't always the tiebreaker that one would expect when multiple tenants are vying for a space. Don't get me wrong, it is increasingly important within our portfolio, but it isn't everything. Often, it is also tenant improvements and capital outlay. Often credit tenants have a larger tenant improvement request than other tenants. In today's leasing environment where immediate make-readies are the standard, picking a tenant with a lower credit profile but an ability to move in immediately without a long, drawn-out, expensive tenant improvement job is a genuine, viable alternative."

Contribute a specific dollar amount rather than commit to a turnkey job where you perform all the work and pay all the costs. Always have tenants contribute their capital first on landlord-provided construction. Make sure you extend the drop-dead date on the delivery of the space if there is any choppiness in the construction material and labor market.

SECURITY DEPOSIT

The landlord holds the up-front payment if the tenant does not honor the lease. The standard amount is equivalent to the last month's rent and operating expenses.

There are several factors when considering the security deposit amount:

- The tenant's credit: The better the credit, the lower the security deposit. Some of the highest-credit tenants in the world do not pay any security deposit. On the flip side, new foreign-owned tenants with sketchy financials often pay four to twelve months of security up front purely based on their lack of track record within the marketplace.

- The amount and type of landlord-funded tenant improvements: You may ask for a larger security deposit if you are coming out of pocket meaningfully to accommodate the tenant. If the type of tenant improvements are highly specialized, unlikely to be used by a future tenant, or costly to remove, you may ask for a higher security deposit.

- The size of the space: Multi-tenant parks, where spaces range from 1,000 to 10,000 square feet, can be in less-than-stellar shape with little incentive to track down and prosecute against a small mom-and-pop type of tenant. Usually, simply asking for a double security deposit is enough to offset any damage you have to deal with while also being a high-enough amount to incentivize the tenant to leave the space in good condition to ensure they receive their deposit back.

- The market cycle: In a soft market, you may be happy to have a tenant lease your space. That doesn't mean they don't have to provide a security deposit, but it does make it less likely that you will have the leverage to ask for an enhanced security deposit.

If you ask for a larger than one-month security deposit (enhanced security deposit), you may be asked to return some of it over time. This is normal and something you are not obligated to do but may warrant consideration. The idea is that with time and good behavior, the tenant can earn your trust by lowering the risk you are facing. It is common to credit an additional security deposit to the tenant's account. Often it is one month per year until only one month remains. This is still all paid up front and is only credited if the tenant is not in default. More on this in the security deposit section of the lease in the next chapter.

Letters of credit (LOC) are security deposit alternatives. Rather than collecting money from the tenant and holding on to it until your tenant has faithfully discharged all of their lease obligations, the tenant's bank can give you a letter of credit. This LOC is an instrument by which the tenant's bank will restrict access to a predetermined amount of the tenant's funds so that they are reserved if the landlord demands payment for a tenant default on the lease.

The main purpose for having a LOC instead of a security deposit is in the event of bankruptcy. In bankruptcy court, tenant security deposits can be protected by the courts and not kept by landlords to discharge the tenant's outstanding financial obligation. On the other hand, with a LOC, the agreement is between the landlord and the tenant's bank, and the landlord can still draw on the letter of credit in case of a simultaneous default and bankruptcy.

GUARANTOR

The guarantor is the entity that will be legally involved if any part of the lease agreement isn't honored. You want to ensure this person or entity is valid and legally authorized to sign on to their role in the lease.

MANAGING MULTIPLE OFFERS

According to DeVonne Boler in Atlanta, "In a balanced marketplace where there is some form of equilibrium between the availability of properties and tenants, most landlords are inclined to deal with tenants and their brokers in a first-come-first-served manner. During the 2020–2022 time frame, though, we often received multiple proposals from creditworthy customers and had to figure out how best to address them." This is where negotiations can turn more into an auction of pitting one group against another or more than one. Some call it a reverse RFP, a bake-off, or an auction. It can be similar to the managed bid process in a competitive investment sale but not as regimented.

This situation gives you a lot of negotiation power. This is where you jockey lease terms between multiple parties to have them bid each other up. Then, in the last phase of the negotiations, you can circumvent the back-and-forth nature of the proposals by creating a final set of terms that can no longer be negotiated and a rigid timeline for a response called a Best and Final.

Write your ideal proposal, send it to the tenants competing for the lease, and say that the first who returns the signed proposal will win. Although this only happens in a very heated marketplace, it is an opportunity to leverage a competitive environment that doesn't create bad blood with the tenants who miss out on the lease should their business come back around in the future.

As Emma Miller of Link Logistics puts it, "When the market is very active, and with low vacancy, your multiple-offer situation might be between an existing tenant and a new tenant. While we always prefer to work with our existing tenants, sometimes you have to put a drop-dead date on negotiations or let the tenant know that if a new tenant signs a lease first, the space is theirs. While we are open and honest with our negotiations and sensitive to the people involved, we must also do what's right for our portfolio."

RENEWALS

The contract is up, and you want to negotiate with the tenant to occupy the building a little longer. When that occurs, you will prepare a letter of intent for them, and the rest of the process is the same as starting from the top of the chapter.

However, you will be dealing with an existing customer, which means treating them as such. This may include giving them better terms to start with. But before the letter of intent phase, feel their desire to stay by informing them you're happy with them and would like to consider a renewal with them. If they respond positively, you can proceed.

You should be the one to kick-start this process. In my experience, tenants begin far too late when they seek renewals with a landlord. Additionally, tenants generally will be less realistic when they initiate and set the first round of negotiation terms. Starting a negotiation with unrealistic terms can create an awkward situation based on having the first negotiation goalpost too far from the realities of the marketplace.

KEY TAKEAWAYS

- A successful property tour includes properly preparing the property and building, ensuring its readiness for inspection, and leaving a positive first impression.
- Maintaining security for a vacant property is essential to prevent theft and vandalism. Consider installing alarms or hiring a security patrol service for larger portfolios.
- After a property tour, brokers should listen for feedback from the tenant to determine whether the building suits their needs and to address any concerns or objections.
- Space planning involves working with a general contractor or space planner to adapt the property to the tenant's specific needs.
- Letters of intent (LOIs) determine if there is enough common ground on business terms before legal fees and time are invested in detailed lease negotiations. Always ensure all terms are agreed upon in the LOI before drafting a lease.
- Managing multiple offers allows landlords to leverage competitive markets for better lease terms.
- Be careful how you manage renewals. Think through how far in advance is appropriate for your current market cycle. Think about how much your capital expenses are going to be to turn the property. And then compare that to the prospect of renewing your existing customer.

NEXT STEPS

You have attracted what you perceive is a great tenant and have terms that might work for both parties. But it all depends on the tenant's financials. How confident are you in their ability to honor the lease? We'll focus on this next so you can make an informed decision on securitization and be prepared to sign the lease.

CHAPTER 8

CREDIT, SECURITIZATION, AND DEAL ANALYSIS

RATE AND CREDIT ARE MOST INVESTORS' PRIMARY focuses. This next step—credit review—is where it pays to get granular. In the eyes of Josh Feinberg, CEO of Otso, a financial services company innovating the credit underwriting and security deposit business for industrial real estate investors, "You have to think of credit review as risk equals rate."

Nicole Welch of Clarion Partners LLC makes what is likely the most important distinction when it comes to credit. "Every investor has its own risk tolerance. When you are vetting credit, you are vetting risk. And while we tend to be more conservative and credit-driven, many fee developers and high-net-worth groups have more flexibility based on their capital expenditure preferences and hold periods to make different trade-offs when balancing rate versus credit." This was never more apparent as when during the 2020–2022 market run-up, newly created third-party logistics companies flooded the market in the search for space. These firms had little to no credit but were flush with cash and willing to pay above-average rental rates with large security deposits and prepaid rents to win leases. Every landlord had to discuss internally where they landed on the risk spectrum regarding whether they would entertain leasing to these groups.

The more you can streamline your application process and have a regimented checklist to assess the tenant's financials, personal financial information when appropriate, and the company's history, the more you can limit the back-and-forth down the road in lease negotiations.

Now, when it comes to the actual credit profile of the tenant, the vast majority of the thirty executives I interviewed for this book, all from the top industrial investment firms across the United States, say the tenant's credit is one of the top criteria, if not *the* top criteria, when they are deciding on who will lease their building.

Granted, you wouldn't do a bad deal with a good tenant just because they have a AAA-rated credit profile, are insanely profitable, and have an impeccable balance sheet. Of course not. But you should prioritize that tenant if it is possible and reasonable to do so. As Bob Andrews of Centerpoint explains, "We would rather do the hard work of a tough negotiation with a credit tenant to land them in our project because once you have invested in that relationship, and in hammering out every single sentence in the lease, you can work on building your long-term relationship with that tenant and find ways to work with them in the future." You should also be more flexible if it helps them choose your building.

Great credit tenants often have needs for multiple buildings. They usually invest heavily within their operation and property, making them sticky and likely to renew. They can sometimes expand within your property's portfolio if you have one. Not only that, but by having a credit tenant in your property, you will achieve better financing terms from banks and get higher valuations and lower cap rates from the capital markets.

So let's walk the path to requesting and reviewing those financials to determine your prospective tenant's creditworthiness. This process depends on the space size and the company you are dealing with.

The smaller, less experienced, private, and newer entities usually provide less vital information, sometimes attempt to withhold information, and tend to have more personal financials backing up the business operation. The larger, more sophisticated, public, and long-held companies have their financials publicly available or are so used to providing financials that a quick call to the CFO is all that is necessary. Then there is the large middle market filled with a blend of these two types of experiences, which is the majority of tenants in the market.

FINANCIALS

Mike Calhoun is the CEO of The Alliance Group, a consultancy focusing exclusively on providing tenant credit assessment reports for landlords. He explains that "the primary financial documents to request are profit and loss statements (P&Ls), balance sheets, and cash-flow statements for larger businesses. For smaller businesses, you will ask for tax returns, personal financial statements, and bank statements. Ideally, you want to see these going back three years and year-to-date (YTD) so you can observe trends."

Be aware that a few circumstances may deviate from the standard process. If the tenant is a public company, you won't need to ask for anything because their financials will be listed on their website in the Investors section under SEC Reporting on their website. This is okay because public companies' financials are audited to ensure they follow all generally accepted accounting principles (GAAP). And the larger the company, the less likely it is that you will receive their tax returns, but instead you will rely solely on their P&L and balance sheet. In about 10 percent of deals, you won't be able to get your eyes on these documents until you sign a non-disclosure agreement (NDA).

CREDIT REVIEW EXPERT

We have plenty of high-net-worth and private-capital clients who have built and sold multiple businesses, leased properties before, and reviewed financials independently. But they are playing with their capital and comfortable taking that risk. Many clients have their own business or personal CPAs reviewing credit and participating in credit interview calls as they are masters of those documents and glean impactful insights.

The larger the landlord, the more likely it is that they will have someone else reviewing the financials to determine creditworthiness. This is because financial statement analysis is a language within the business community that few people speak. So who do you have on the finance team who can review financials for you? Usually, it is your CFO, CPA, or chief credit officer. Most landlords are also fiduciaries of an investor's capital and, as a result, must ensure they do everything in their power to protect investors' capital.

Most asset managers and leasing directors are relieved to have a qualified expert within their firm, or hired by their firm, to handle credit analysis because it frees them up to do what they do best: taking care of the property.

So ask yourself, "Should I be responsible for reviewing this tenant's credit? Do I have enough experience and expertise needed to do a great job?" If not, who do you know internally who is the most likely fit? Is your CPA available and capable if you don't have an internal resource? If not, who does your attorney or broker know who can help? What third-party credit analysis groups can you work with to review credit?

CREDIT ANALYSIS

The first challenge is creating a standardized process. The second challenge is the collection of financials, as small, medium, and large private firms provide disaggregated, often piecemeal, unaudited financials.

I wouldn't say I love reviewing and analyzing financials, but I have a master's in business administration from the University of Southern California, where I took financial statement analysis and financial accounting. It was a memorable time because I finished my final project on my honeymoon from a hotel in Cape Town, South Africa, to graduate on time.

These are the first three things you should look at:

- Revenue trends: Is gross revenue increasing or decreasing? How sharply or subtly are they trending? What revenue segments are affected?
- Real estate expenses as a percentage of revenue: The general rule of thumb in real estate is that 5 percent to 8 percent of a tenant's total gross revenue accounts for their lease. If the rent being contemplated is greater, you should inquire to understand this risk and adjust your security deposit accordingly.
- Real estate expenses compared to the last location: Tenants are known to increase their facilities and overhead incrementally. Doubling overhead spend or size is common, but tripling is rare and cause for concern.

After those simple items, I review several of the following:

- Subsidiary level financials for tenants owned by a larger parent company: Hayes Graham of Terreno reiterates an important part on entities: "How the tenant's firm's entities roll up to the corporate entity is extremely important. You may think you are ultimately getting the corporate parent's credit when you are not. You need to see a streamlined version of the ownership profile linking to the parent credit."
- Debt coverage ratios
- Debt maturities, interest rates, and choke points
- Taxable net operating income trends
- EBITDA margin trends
- Auditor statement footnotes

Mike Calhoun of The Alliance Group reminds us that when thinking about tenant businesses, we must be mindful that "every industry market niche is different in terms of margins, growth rates, and need for debt. This makes it unhelpful to apply cookie-cutter financial guidelines."

Assessing a credit review is a safety net for the investment's soundness and gives you a place to negotiate. If uncertain about their credit, you can charge them a premium rent to mitigate your risk.

Josh Feinberg, CEO of Otso, explains, "Our clients told us they struggled with unaudited financial data that was often incomplete. To solve for this we created a platform that enables connection to bank accounts as well as deep credit reporting systems. Armed with this data, we utilize AI and machine-learning algorithms to analyze daily balances, transfers, and credit/payment histories over two years to weigh and score the applicants. This creates a comprehensive (and accurate) financial profile and gives a landlord a sense of what they are likely to experience with that tenant."

TENANT INTERVIEW

Rarely do landlords want, need, or think to have a call with the prospective tenant to discuss their financials. The financial discussion call with tenants is one of the most insightful actions to learn about your future tenant, build rapport, and, more importantly, reduce your risk. Reading financials doesn't tell the story of the business.

These are my favorite questions to ask prospective tenants:

- Revenue
  - How many customers do you have?
  - Who are your largest customers?
  - What share of your total revenue do those customers represent?
  - What do the agreements you sign with your top customers look like?
- Expense
  - What are your largest variable and fixed expenses?
  - How have they changed as you've grown?
  - What do your receivables look like?

- Debt
  - When is your next largest debt obligation maturity?
- Labor
  - How are you dealing with the challenging labor markets?
- Transportation
  - How often do you ship and receive products?
  - Where are your products coming from?
  - Where are you shipping them to?
- Equipment
  - What equipment purchases will you be making for this property?
- Geography
  - Why do business here?
- Economic
  - How are you dealing with the economic environment?

These open-ended questions will tell you everything you need to know to supplement your internal or external credit review. These questions will also give you a good feel for how your prospective tenant does business, their concerns, their aspirations, and the robustness of their business. The investment is thirty minutes, and learning more about your tenant-to-be has no downside risk. This will likely be one of the last interactions or new information you receive before making a go-or-no-go decision on leasing to this prospective tenant.

SITE VISIT

When in doubt, ask to visit your prospective tenant's current location to see their operation with your own two eyes. Usually, this is most helpful for tenants with over 20,000 square feet where there is more variation in the actual operation of the company. Meeting your prospective tenant at their building and walking it with them will likely teach you everything you need to give you an opinion on all matters of the leasing process, when you may not yet have enough information on paper to judge their worthiness. That's how Bob Andrew of Centerpoint likes to do things. "Getting into the field," he says, "and shaking the hands of the decision maker and their team, whenever practical, is invaluable. Knowing who they are, their values, how they handle themselves and their organization, and walking their building with them will impact our final decision of whom we select as our tenant."

SECURITY DEPOSIT

Now that you have collected, analyzed, interviewed, and inspected your tenant, you must determine how much security to require. First, you should assess the break-even point of your out-of-pocket expenses. Then you can consider your credit assessment and determine the amount necessary.

Most landlords simply ask for one month of rent unless there are red flags in a cursory review of financials. Some landlords of small multi-tenant shallow bay projects ask for two months as a standard to protect their lower break-even point. Many landlords ask for a three-to-six-month security deposit if they deal with a new business on a sizable building. Occasionally more sophisticated landlords will ask for these security deposits to be in the form of a letter of credit to protect from bankruptcy proceedings. And now, insurance bonds are available that you claim in the event of default.

If you choose the insurance bond, the tenant must pay for the bond issued in your name. Then if in the future there is a default, you provide notice to the insurance company of the default and notice after the end of the cure period. The insurance then pays the security claim to the beneficiary, the landlord, and starts the legal process with the tenant.

Now, you can benchmark your tenant's creditworthiness against the deal.

ECONOMICS REVIEW AND ASSESSMENT

When you receive a proposal from a tenant, a primary point of concern is the economic review of its terms. What are their proposals worth to you?

To answer, start at a baseline review by comparing your budget with what the potential tenants are offering, and determine which proposal is closest. That's the simple assessment, and if you have prepared a budget, you will already have taken a moment to assess what is important to you and your view of the market. Industrial investors usually have a specific strategy around maximizing cash flow or asset value. Depending on the marketplace and capital markets, the same landlord can shift their strategy over time. The tools and frameworks below can help you determine which proposal maximizes which metric.

After that, you will find that a complex wrinkle can arise because tenant proposals vary wildly. Their subtle nuances force you to ask yourself tough questions about your needs. Consider these two hypothetical lease proposals for the same space:

- Tenant 1—Five years firm term. Two months of free rent. One-hundred-thousand dollars in TI. Marginal credit profile.
- Tenant 2—Seven years firm term. Six months of free rent. Twenty-thousand dollars in TI. Long-standing private company.

When facing high variability in proposals such as the above examples, build a matrix to compare data side by side. How will you decide which option is better? Generally speaking, you want to be keenly aware of a few things. First, note your up-front costs. Next, how much are you recouping on earnings in rent per year over the total contract? After that, evaluate the likelihood that they will honor their commitments. With this information known, there are fewer surprises. You can pick which one aligns more closely with your business philosophies. On top of that, you can also use this matrix to adjust your responses to the tenant proposals.

After you make your counteroffers, they will respond in kind. With the new offers, you can then input their variabilities again to keep track of their trading, negotiation style, and if they operate in good faith.

Further assisting in your decisions, these data points help you determine "net effective rent." This amount is 1) the total amount of rent (over the life of the lease), 2) subtracted by the number of concessions that are given, which then needs to be 3) divided by the number of years in the lease's term. The resulting number gives you a $/SF/year rate. That metric helps you compare the highly variable proposals and puts them on equal terms.

Remember that if you have multiple offers over multiple rounds of negotiation, each round should improve your competitive position. Track whether or not that's true by recording the metrics for all rounds.

When reviewing lease deal economics, there are various methods, from the back of the napkin to Excel to web-based applications. We use VTS almost exclusively to ensure we are moving in lockstep with our institutional investment landlord partners while also elevating the client experience for our high-net-worth clients.

Below is an example of a deal analysis when comparing a lease proposal with the budget for the space. The second-order analysis will include reviewing competing proposals against one another and the budget. The last level of analysis will include multiple rounds of negotiations with multiple parties if it comes to that. The idea here is to compare your budget against other proposals and then see progress throughout the negotiation to achieve superior results.

PROPOSAL ANALYSIS

The definitions for NER and NPV are as follows:

NER ($/SF/YR): Net effective rent (NER) represents the sum of all monthly cash flow, inclusive of total rental, recovery, and

PROPOSAL

OVERVIEW	BUDGET	LANDLORD
Label	001 Q1 2022	Full Bldg 61 Months
Date Entered	12/31/21	03/15/22
Lease Type	Triple Net	Triple Net
Type	—	NEW
Space (s)	001	001
Size (sq.f)	45,795	47,287
Downtime (mo)	—	—
Tenant Possession Date	—	04/01/22
LCD		04/01/22
Term (mo)	60	61

INCOME	BUDGET	LANDLORD
Base Rent	$11.40	1–12: $16.80 13–24: $17.47 25–36: $18.17 37–48: $18.89 49–60: $19.65 61–61: $20.44
Escalations	—	—
Recoveries ($/SF/YR)	$0.0	$3.72
Total Other Income ($/SF/YR)	$0.0	$0.0

CONCESSIONS	BUDGET	LANDLORD
Free Rent	1–1:100%, Gross	2–2:100%, Net
Total Free Rent	$43,505.25	$66,200.40
Tenant Improvements ($/SF)	$1.0	$0.0
Building Improvements ($/SF)	$0.0	$0.0
Commissions	1–60:$154,008.59 LR	1–60: 2.5% Net TR 61–61: 2.5% Net TR 1–60: 2.5% Net TR 61–61: 1.25% Net TR
Total Commissions	$154,008.59	$213,856.32
Concessions ($/SF)	$5.31	$5.92

EXPENSE	BUDGET	LANDLORD
Total Expenses ($/SF/YR)	$0.0	$3.72

OPTIONS AND RIGHTS	BUDGET	LANDLORD
Type(s)		—

METRICS	BUDGET	LANDLORD
NER ($/SF/YR)	$10.18	$17.07
NER vs. Last Offer		—
NER vs. Budget		**67.7%**
NPV ($/SF)	$43.82	$86.77

other income, less all concessions, remaining lease obligations, and tenant share of building expenses, discounted monthly over the term of the lease.

NPV ($/SF): Net present value (NPV) is the value of the proposal amortized over the lease term monthly using the discount rate specified multiplied by twelve. Total NPV is divided by the rentable size of the lease.

CASH-FLOW ANALYSIS

The cash-flow analysis is another tool within VTS that we leverage. The idea here is that, as terms are input throughout the process of proposals through to fully executed lease, they are tracked, forecasted, and reported in ways that can make the analysis and context faster and easier for landlords to understand their up-front costs (e.g., tenant improvements and leasing commissions), and to audit their lease economics to ensure that they are calculated correctly.

As with Excel models and Argus DCF analysis, you can have calculation errors; however, with software like VTS, they are quicker to find and correct. One multibillion-dollar private equity fund asset manager further clarifies, "We have different investment vehicles with different objectives. For the cash-flow-oriented investors, we will start the lease renewal process earlier to start the conversation to help minimize downtime. For funds that are more IRR driven, we might be willing to take downtime exposure if doing so allows us to sign a new lease with a higher residual value." Here you can use VTS to help you make more nuanced underwriting value judgments.

Lastly, with VTS, we can implement process workflows and dependencies. These features allow asset managers and brokers to increase their quality control by limiting the ability of a proposal to go to an executed lease without all of the proper approvals, disclosures, and requirements. This can help with institutional investors' internal auditing and controls and even help high-net-worth investors improve their processes and procedures as they scale.

Deal Terms

Rentable size	47,286	Lease Term	61 mo.
Commencement	04/01/22	Expiration	04/30/27
Lease Type	Triple Net	Base Rent	$66,200.40
Free Rent	1 mo.	Tenant Improvements	$0.00
Building Improvements	$0.00	Other Fees	$0.00
Tenant Commissions	$106,928.16	Landlord Commissions	$106,928.16
Real Estate Taxes	$0.00	Opex	$3.72

Cash Flow Chart

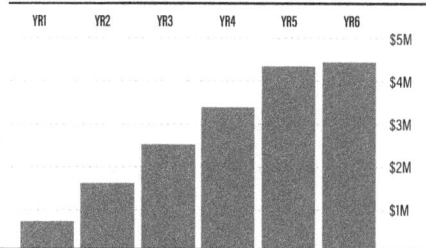

Cash Flow

	NPV (0%)	Total	YR 1	YR 2	YR 3	YR 4	YR 5	YR 6
Start Date			4/2022	4/2023	4/2024	4/2025	4/2026	4/2027
Base Rent	$4,383,056	$4,383,056	$794,404.80	$826,181.04	$859,228.20	$893,357.40	$929,341.20	$80,542.91
Abated Base Rent	(66,200)	(66,200)	(66,200)	0.00	0.00	0.00	0.00	0.00
Opex Recovery	894,178.26	894,178.26	175,903.92	175,903.92	175,903.92	175,903.92	175,903.92	14,658.66
Abated Recoveries	0.00	0.00	0.00	0.00	0.00	0.00	0.00	0.00
Gross Revenue	5,211,033	5,211,033	904,108	1,002,085	1,035,132	1,069,261	1,105,245	95,202
Opex	(894,178.26)	(894,178.26)	(175,903.92)	(175,903.92)	(175,903.92)	(175,903.92)	(175,903.92)	(14,658.66)
Total Expenses	(894,178.26)	(894,178.26)	(175,903.92)	(175,903.92)	(175,903.92)	(175,903.92)	(175,903.92)	(14,658.66)
Net Operating Income	$4,316,855.15	$4,316,855.15	$728,204.40	$826,181.04	$859,228.20	$893,357.40	$929,341.20	$80,542.91
Commissions	(213,856.32)	(213,856.32)	(213,856.32)	0.00	0.00	0.00	0.00	0.00
Net Cash Flow	$4,316,855.15	$4,316,855.15	$728,204.40	$826,181.04	$859,228.20	$893,357.40	$929,341.20	$80,542.91

Best of all, these reports are exported to Excel and PDF, and they can be shared internally with all necessary parties.

One institutional investor who owns 30 million square feet of Class A industrial space within Southern California explained, "We don't look at NPV at all because we don't offer concessions or TIs and just focus on base starting rate and try to maximize what is available within the market." Where you land on the spectrum of deal analysis will depend on your portfolio, team, tools, and relationship with your capital partners. Sometimes, your analysis is as simple as the NOI created by the lease.

KEY TAKEAWAYS

- Credit review is crucial in industrial real estate investments, as it helps assess a tenant's financial risk and creditworthiness. When making decisions, investors must consider their risk tolerance and balance rate against credit.
- A standardized credit review process involves analyzing financial documents, conducting tenant interviews, and potentially visiting a tenant's current location. Key factors include revenue trends, real estate expenses, debt coverage ratios, and financial stability.
- Determining an appropriate security deposit is essential in managing financial risk. Factors to consider include break-even points, credit assessment, and the use of insurance bonds, letters of credit, or other financial instruments to protect the landlord in case of default.
- Start by comparing your budget with potential tenants' proposals and determine which is closest.
- Be aware that tenant proposals can vary widely and require careful consideration.
- Build a matrix to compare data side by side, considering up-front costs, rent earnings, and the likelihood of commitment.
- Use "net effective rent" (NER) and "net present value" (NPV) as key metrics to compare proposals.
- Track the progress of multiple offers and negotiations to maintain a competitive position.
- Utilize tools like VTS for streamlined analysis of lease deal economics, cash-flow analysis, and proposal tracking.

- Implement process workflows and dependencies in VTS to maintain quality control and meet internal audit requirements.
- Be aware that you may focus on different metrics depending on your portfolio, team, tools, and capital partners at the time.

NEXT STEPS

Now, you have the tools to reel in the tenant of your choosing under terms that suit you and them, and you know they can back up their end of the agreement. You've done 80 percent of the work by this point. But as my favorite partner, Scott Smith, in our Phoenix office light-heartedly reminds me, "Don't go to the Porsche dealership just yet." A signed LOI with a credit tenant means the deal is yours to lose. Now is the time to close.

CHAPTER 9

LEASE NEGOTIATIONS

YOU'RE IN THE HOME STRETCH AFTER YOU CAN NEGO-tiate terms that both parties are happy with, and you feel confident your potential tenants can pay rent. Depending on how complex things are, you can use an AIR-style document that helps you fill in the blanks. Or you can ensure everything is airtight by using a trained and seasoned lawyer.

I've heard stories from generations back that boilerplate leases were once two pages, and I've seen leases from twenty years ago that were six pages. When I first entered the business, they had grown to nine pages. Now, though, we see sizes anywhere between fifteen and sixty pages.

Lease agreements are growing because they add more complexity that warrants more protections. Over time, things have happened that created new mechanisms to prevent those things from happening again.

Further, it's not as if the relationship ends when the tenant moves in. You and they will be joined for the next ten years, and language needs to account for critical dates or possible catastrophes to consider within that long time frame. If your tenant disposes of chemicals once daily, there are then 3,650 chances during the lease term where there could be a nasty spill, and the lease agreement best prepares both parties for that and many other possibilities.

It's a document that structures your relationship with the tenant, carving out the rights and responsibilities of both parties. Regardless of the direction you choose—boilerplate or custom—there are several lease terms to understand to ensure a successful agreement.

LEASE AGREEMENTS

The general sentiment for commercial real estate contracts is that properties and asset types are so unique that having one uniform contract wouldn't be feasible. You have offices, industrial buildings, multi-family, hotels, self-storage, medical offices, etc. These building types have differences and nuances that require leases to be tailored to the situation. To accomplish these needs, there are form contracts and custom contracts.

Usually, we will find high-net-worth investors using the broker-modified AIR forms with slight attorney modification. In contrast, most institutional investors have big law lease agreements crafted to suit their unique needs. What is suitable for your needs?

FORM CONTRACTS

Form contracts are prewritten or standardized contracts that can be applied and adjusted to a specific deal. Some argue that form contracts create efficiency in executing agreements by establishing industry norms that end last-second negotiations and gotchas.

A group called AIR (American Industrial Real Estate) exists in Southern California, and like the National Association of Realtors, AIR has numerous form contracts for use in all commercial property situations. Their lease agreements are balanced and reputable, and both parties generally feel that the contract content represents the interests of everybody in a balanced manner. AIR contracts are not in every state, but each state's NAR usually has its form if you are in a pinch.

The advantage of using a form contract is to save time and money. You won't have to take the time to try to find, contract with, wait for drafting, or wait for comment turnaround, or pay thousands of dollars. You also won't receive practical advice from a seasoned legal professional. No dollar size will dictate whether or not to use a form contract. We have used AIR lease contracts on leases valued at multiple million dollars per year. What changes are the complexities of a deal and the need to change terms from the AIR lease.

The mechanics of filling out an AIR document are usually that the broker fills out the contract form with all the pertinent deal points spelled out within the LOI. Then the landlord can review it and send it to their attorney to review. In that review, the attorney is on the clock to start thinking about practical risks and mitigations.

I recommend *AIR Commercial Real Estate Forms: A User's Manual, Volume 1: Lease Forms and Addenda*, written by John L. Pagliassotti and Richard L. Riemer, Esq, and edited by Timothy Hayes. This book was written by the people who wrote the AIR lease, published its regular updates, and provided helpful insights for each clause. This is another excellent reference manual for you if you like the simplicity of the AIR contract for your properties.

CUSTOM CONTRACTS

The alternative to form contracts is custom contracts, which are customarily drawn up by the landlord's attorney. The broker provides the landlord with the fully agreed-upon LOI, and the attorneys draft the lease. This might be from scratch or, more likely, from a prior form with that client or a previous document from their practice.

Now there is an advantage in being the party that draws up the lease as you set the tone for every right and responsibility for the relationship. Most attorneys already have the forms they use as templates and customize from.

Use a custom-drawn lease if you have specific initiatives in your real estate operating company that you want to ensure flow through your lease documents. For Prologis, this is the Clear Lease that deals with prepaying and capping operating expenses, which is unique to their model. Other institutional investors now have environmental, sustainability, and governance (ESG) language.

I recommend *The Lease Manual: A Practical Guide to Negotiating Office, Retail, and Industrial Leases* by April F. Condon with

Rodney J. Dillman, Second Edition, which is released by the American Bar Association's Real Property Trust and Estate Law Section. It is the most user-friendly manual for explaining lease clauses and provides each clause's landlord, tenant, broker, and lender perspectives. It is a must-have for the bookshelf of any serious investor or practitioner constantly parsing lease language. It is a 529-page book!

CLEAR LEASE

Prologis has been a trailblazer in all aspects of industrial real estate. Among many notable innovations is the Clear Lease. What is it? It is as close to a short and straightforward lease as it gets while remaining robust enough to deal with Fortune 100 tenants. The main change here is that Prologis took care of all operating and capital repair expenses and capped them by a certain percentage. That then allows the rest of the contract to be shorter and more straightforward.

Craig Viergiver of Lee & Associates' Atlanta office echoes many of the industry's tenants: "Landlords can aid the speed at which they can do business with great tenants by having a shorter lease form. The Clear Lease addresses this problem of nitpicking every CapEx item in the lease and all the extra time and money spent on legal fees. Operations people love this."

ATTORNEYS

Should you use an outside attorney or in-house counsel? Should you use the same firm or attorney for all your leases? Should you have your asset managers select their attorneys based on experience, relationship, and geography? Every investor has their take on this topic.

There is a fairly typical arc that people experience from the moment they enter commercial real estate that evolves as they gain experience. At the start, nobody thinks they need an attorney. They're too expensive, the thinking goes. Or, they'll have a cousin who's an attorney who will give them the family rate.

Over time, you recognize the value of a great real estate–specific attorney. Great attorneys are sensitive to billing their clients, are judicious in spending time only on top priorities, and meaningfully protect against your most impactful risks.

The question emerges, How do you tell the difference between good and bad attorneys? The industry saying inside the legal community from young associate attorneys is "find them, bind them, and grind them." I say this tongue in cheek. The takeaway is that attorneys only have their time and expertise to sell to the marketplace. They recognize that and must ensure they sell their time as best they can. They will spend as much time as you require, but you must also understand what is worth their time. A great attorney knows and guards against spending time on low-value-add legal work. Great attorneys want to fill their time with the highest-impact work.

Another red flag for a bad attorney is if they have a big ego. Attorneys are people, too, of course. As Ryan Holiday describes in *Ego Is the Enemy*, "Impressing people is utterly different from being truly impressive." You want an empathetic attorney focused on you and your needs, not on them and their showmanship.

Lastly, you want an attorney who will be responsive. Some attorneys will undercommunicate, tell you to be patient, or be non-responsive. We are all busy people in this business. But being too busy to communicate is selfish. Being too busy is okay if you set expectations and only work on assignments where you can accomplish the needed work. If you are not prioritized, your deal may fall through. Remember the mantra we learned on day one in the commercial real estate brokerage business, "time kills all deals."

Good attorneys, in contrast, will know what's important to you and what's not and how to accomplish your priorities promptly and efficiently. Although attorneys benefit financially from their work, good attorneys perform for the client they represent and gel with the broker representing the client rather than stacking hours for their benefit.

If they are unsure how their client might feel about a specific detail in the contract, a good lawyer will check in with the client to solicit their preferences. Good attorneys work as an extension of you and will seek your advice on proceeding with their aggressive, mediocre, or passive approach.

A good attorney will also work with the client to create a priority list and work toward ensuring the biggest needs are met. Additionally, lawyers can be so good that they'll recognize when your deal is less sophisticated and does not require a fine-toothed comb. They will then push it down onto their lower-rate associates to help save you money rather than run up the tab.

When you find a great attorney, just like a great broker, lender, or anyone else in your personal and professional network, hang on to them! The fruits of your labor have an exponential effect as time passes, and you can better work together based on your shared experience.

If you receive a recommendation for an attorney during your search, my only advice is to research their specialty. You should be looking for somebody who primarily deals with real estate. While vetting them, ask them about the most recent deals they worked on that are similar to yours.

You must also realize that your attorney is not responsible for living with the negotiated and agreed-to lease. You are. You cannot rely on your attorney to know everything important to you. Here, sophisticated investors excel at directing and collaborating with their attorneys to have them weigh in on high-impact clauses and issues and then work through the other issues internally.

NEGOTIATING LEASE TERMS

Remember, your broker is not an attorney and isn't qualified to understand any level of protection the contract may or may not offer. Brokers know this. Brokers don't want to be liable for advice they give within the lease agreement. Brokers can often be put into a bad position if their client asks for advice on the lease agreement and isn't investing in an attorney reviewing and negotiating on their behalf.

As a rule, the smaller and less sophisticated the deal, the more the brokers can complete a form contract and act as the master of ceremonies. They can forward these documents to the lawyers when they fill out dates and amounts. Any issue that arises and calls for lawyers to negotiate is usually relatively simple.

However, with custom-drawn leases, you usually will find that as the lease agreement develops, the final finer legal points will be negotiated between the attorneys on either side of the transaction. Once the attorneys come on the scene, they often will speak to each other on behalf of their clients.

Custom contracts create sophistication and complexity, usually calling for multiple conversations between attorneys. Usually, they will discuss the major issues. Clients typically aren't privy to those conversations and should assume their lawyer is working optimally on their behalf.

As the negotiation draws closer, brokers and their clients get involved again if there are more nuanced conversations and when a conference or meeting needs to be called to hash out the final details. Attorneys will still be present to take ownership of the legal language and interpretation of the protections, rights, and responsibilities being parsed.

I write this section as a guide for what to think and look for in a lease agreement. Remember, I am not an attorney. This is not legal advice. I have, however, looked at more than six hundred leases and have a high-level understanding of the majority of topics within the lease.

PARTIES

Who are you legally allowed to go after if the tenant does not perform and uphold the responsibilities of the lease? The legal entity that is written in this section of the contract. Make sure this entity is valid, that it is the same entity whose financials you recently reviewed, and that it is licensed to do business in the state where the property is located.

To do this, you can quickly double-check with the Secretary of State website that the entity that intends to sign the lease is valid. If it is not, stop and do not proceed until you find a resolution. The idea here is to ensure you can enforce your rights within the lease contract if necessary in a court of law.

We see this all the time in Southern California with new entities based overseas and principals that are not US citizens. They may have money in the bank and provide a healthy security deposit that offsets your risk by leasing to them. Still, you only do this if you understand that your ability to enforce the lease is unlikely.

SQUARE FOOTAGE

This describes the size of the space being leased. Square footage is an approximation. According to the BOMA standard, you can hire five architects to measure your building and still come up with modest differences. Make sure there is some sort of disclaimer that the square footage of the building is an approximation. Furthermore, make sure your disclaimer states that the tenant is conscious that the amount of money they pay each month for rent is independent of the size of the building. Your attorney can guide you here.

The last thing you want is for a tenant to say that they measured the building themselves, that the building is smaller than advertised, and that they will only pay the dollar-per-square-foot rent based on what they measured. This is an inexperienced tenant ploy, but surprisingly, inexperienced tenants can be in 2,000, 20,000, or 200,000 square feet as the business may not be new, but the people managing it who are responsible for the lease decisions are.

DATES

Dates and dollars go hand in hand. Any delay in dates usually comes with a delay in rent collection. That doesn't always apply, though certain time frames outside the landlord's control should be bracketed with a drop-dead date, like in tenant-performed improvements. And even more importantly, you want to ensure that your tenant is clear on when the lease term commences and when the rent commences. One in every twenty tenants gets confused here or tries to work ambiguity to their advantage. The lease agreement has several important dates to isolate and clarify.

- **Rent Commencement Date:** The date that the tenant is to start paying rent.
- **Operating Expenses Date:** The date that the tenant is to start paying the operating expenses.
- **Early Possession Date:** When the tenant can start moving furniture, fixtures, and equipment into the building but not operate their business.
- **Possession Date:** The date the tenant can fully utilize the property.
- **Drop Dead Date:** If delays in possession move past this date, the lease can be terminated.

Be very clear about all of the above dates. Make sure you communicate these dates openly with the tenant. Inexperienced tenants may come with a whole host of different expectations. It is not uncommon for inexperienced tenants to do the following:

- Try to push out the date when the rent starts and then push up the date they get possession.
- Move in and start operating their business the second they get keys to the space.
- Think that they don't have to pay the operating expenses during a month when they have free rent.
- Don't expect to pay rent until their landlord performs tenant improvements.

Possession can be important to clarify, too, and it is often listed as "upon substantial completion of construction" instead of as a specific date. You ideally want it to be on a specific day regardless of the completion of tenant improvements. This issue can be stressful, as construction can be delayed for countless reasons. It could be because of something within the landlord's or tenant's control or something outside anybody's control, like supply chain disruptions, equipment shortages, labor strikes, congestion at the ports, or many other factors. It usually is from the tenant spending extra time designing the space, value engineering the project, and approving to get started with the work. As the landlord, you don't want to forgo being paid rent for an extended time and must manage this risk if you are managing tenant improvements.

Clarifying these dates eliminates possible confusion. Many of these issues don't happen in strong landlord markets. But in soft markets, these happen with regularity. The difference here is in cash flow. You can protect your cash flow by being clear on these dates.

TOTAL DUE UPON EXECUTION / PREPAID RENT

This is the amount of money due when you execute the lease. For starters, a lease is not legally valid until both parties have signed the agreement and money has changed hands. You do not want to sign the lease until you have the check. You also don't want to sign the lease until the check has cleared. Once you have the signed lease from the tenant and their check has cleared, you can countersign the lease, which consummates the lease transaction.

Secondly, you want to ensure that it is evident what amount of money the tenant pays when signing the lease. Some of the most expensive, biggest law firm contracts spell out all the dates and dollars and then leave the tenant scratching their head at how much they make their payment and whom to pay. Call out exactly how much is due and where to send the money. Ideally, now in the age of digital payments, it is ACH or wire, meaning you will need to provide those instructions. If not in the lease, then make a cover letter that welcomes the tenant as a customer and provides them with all of the relevant information needed to execute the lease, make their payment, and connect with their property manager.

FREE RENT

For starters, specify which month rent will be abated. Secondly, operating expenses are not abated during this free-rent period.

You'll want to consider how any free rent affects the rent schedule. For example, have annual escalations be twelve months after commencement instead of twelve months after rent payment has begun.

There should also be a stipulation in the lease agreement that if the tenant defaults, any free rent given is not only paid back but is due immediately. This is a great way to ensure that if you incentivize the tenant to lease your property, they must honor their commitments before taking advantage of the incentive.

SECURITY DEPOSIT

This is a quick reminder for those new to the industry or those who own a multi-family property. The security deposit is never used as the last month's rent and operating expense, even though it is equivalent to that amount.

When it comes to securitizing the lease, not only is credit a primary driver of the security deposit amount, but so is the amount of up-front out-of-pocket expenses that the landlord contributes in tenant improvements and leasing commissions.

An enhanced deposit is greater than one month's rent and protects the landlord against assessed risk. Ask for an enhanced security deposit as often as practical. I ask for a double security deposit on all spaces under 10,000 square feet, knowing that if a tenant doesn't fulfill their lease obligations in a small property, they are unlikely to be around when it comes time to restore the property. If a tenant does not have a track record or does not have citizenship, ask for two to six months minimum.

You can also structure enhanced security deposits to burn off over time. The tenant will get part of their deposit back incrementally for good behavior, usually one month per year.

Lastly, consider a letter of credit with larger leases, as letters of credit are exempt from bankruptcy proceedings in most jurisdictions. And as Bob Andrews of Centerpoint reminds us, "Make sure the term of the letter of credit is longer than the lease so that you have an opportunity to remedy any deficiency in the surrender and restoration of the premises upon lease expiration."

WARRANTY

Do you want to guarantee that everything in your building is perfectly new and will work forever? Of course not. With the AIR lease form, the default is that all building systems will be warrantied for thirty days and that the HVAC units will be warrantied for the first six months. After that, they are the sole responsibility of the tenant. The idea here is that it is not practical for a tenant to hire inspectors to inspect every space they intend to lease, and they are not buying the building. This short warranty period assures tenants that they can lease a property with as little as one or two tours and be confident that the landlord will hand off a building with all the systems in proper working order.

With each passing day, however, these warranty periods are lessening. It is more typical now in custom-drawn lease agreements to see a blanket statement that says by taking possession of the space, the tenant is accepting the property's condition.

You get to choose what approach you want to take here. Usually, I see landlords service all of the building systems and then not provide any warranty. The idea here is that once the building systems are in the hands of the tenant, the tenant is in control of them, and the amount to which they use, and potentially overuse, specific components of the systems is up to them.

MAINTENANCE, REPAIR, AND REPLACEMENT

Operating expenses can be further broken down into maintenance, repair, and replacement. Maintenance, repair, and replacement are often part of operating and capital expenses, which could be a redundant section of the lease agreement that only applies in some situations. But there are often nuances in how these expenses come about that change the triggered proportions of responsibility.

The first part of this section is to identify further who is responsible for performing maintenance, repairs, and replacement of which items. The second part concerns the mechanics of budgets, payments, and reimbursements, and the third concerns amortization as needed.

Be intentional about how you want to run your operations as an investor. Do you want to be hands-on and build a team to handle maintenance issues to ensure the highest level of service? Do you want to be hands-off, have your tenants do everything, try to enforce compliance, and make up for deficiencies? Most landlords prefer to be hands-off, so they want to offload as much as possible onto their tenants, with Prologis being the main exception.

CAPITAL EXPENSES

The roof, load-bearing walls, foundation, and HVAC units—these are the capital expense items that are most hotly contested between landlords and tenants. Most industrial leases during my career have the landlord responsible for these items. There is momentum to shift these items onto the tenant as tenants have exclusive control of these systems during their occupancy in most instances. Of course, tenants still think they should not be responsible for large capital items of someone else's buildings. You'll want to think through your take on these primary building systems.

INSURANCE

When negotiating the insurance section of an industrial real estate lease as a landlord, there are several vital points to consider. Firstly, the tenant must pay for your insurance through operating expense reimbursements and provide their general liability insurance policy. The lease should specify what insurance the tenant requires, the amount, and coverage limits. Generally, the total amount of insurance coverage should exceed the worst-case or multi-accident scenario for your building.

In addition to general liability and property insurance, the lease should address what other types of insurance the tenant must carry, such as product liability, cyber liability, or flood insurance, depending on the nature of their business and the property's location. The tenant must provide proof of insurance, and the lease should specify how and when this must be provided.

The lease should also require the tenant to list you as an additional insured on their insurance policy and waive their right of subrogation against you. Additionally, it should specify how and when the tenant must notify you of any claims or incidents that could lead to a claim and how deductibles and self-insured retentions will be handled.

You want to be notified as soon as possible so you can take appropriate action to protect your interests.

The lease should address what happens if the tenant fails to maintain the required insurance coverage, including whether you have the right to terminate the lease and are entitled to any remedies or damages if the tenant causes a loss or damage not covered by insurance.

Addressing these factors can help ensure that you and your tenant are adequately protected in an accident or loss.

INDEMNIFICATION

Mutual indemnification has been the most hotly contested term in the lease contract throughout the last ten years, and most landlords don't provide it, not even for preexisting hazardous materials. If you will indemnify the tenant mutually, ensure that you don't offer reciprocal indemnity, because the tenant controls their premises and the common area.

HAZARDOUS SUBSTANCES

The lease will deal with the property condition related to hazardous substances. Important for your liability, you will want to be able to prove that the property was clean when you handed it over to the tenant. That way, if a problem happens on-site, you will be protected. For Bob Andrews of Centerpoint Properties, "The biggest sticking point is always environmental. Our investment strategy is predicated on being in infill markets close to the ports and transportation nodes, and this happens to be where there are environmental issues from prior uses. Whether it's Los Angeles, Oakland, Seattle, or Chicago, there is usually an environmental component to deal with preexisting conditions."

The challenge with environmental concerns is delineating between one property and another and between past, present, and future issues. No landlord wants their tenant to release a hazardous substance on their property. Equally, no tenant wants to be responsible for a prior tenant or neighbor's hazardous substance release. And landlords and tenants alike want to avoid being liable for hazardous substance releases that migrated from neighboring properties.

If there is any material concern about a dangerous existing issue, consider an environmental site assessment to measure the baseline conditions before occupancy. Additionally, you don't want any of your environmental issues to cause safety concerns to your tenants, which can usually be mitigated by indoor air testing if there are subsurface vapor concerns.

SUBLEASE, ASSIGNMENT, AND RECAPTURE

If the tenant no longer needs the building during their lease term, they can sublease, or you can recapture the property. Subleasing involves the tenant finding a new occupant, receiving rent from this third party, and then paying you as a fulfillment of the original lease agreement. In a sublease situation, the tenant must jump through all the hoops previously discussed in this book. Then you can reasonably approve or deny any third-party tenant based on legitimate property risks and their credit.

Another way to prevent third-party tenants is to recapture. Recapturing involves taking back possession of the space. In most instances, language in the lease can state your right to take the property back if the tenant seeks to sublease all or a portion of the property for the remainder of the lease term.

Recapture is usually beneficial in strong markets because it allows you to find a new creditworthy tenant at a potentially higher lease rate. If the market is down, you will usually delay using recapture and instead enable the tenant to continue being responsible for backfilling their space through a sublease.

If you choose not to recapture or do not have that right, you should at least make sure to have a profit-sharing provision. The most common profit-sharing split is 50/50 between landlord and tenant, with some institutional investors splitting it 60/40. The idea here is that in a market upswing, where rates are increasing, a tenant may be able to sublease the space for more than they are paying.

The concept of profit sharing disincentivizes the tenant from seeking profit in leasing their space. You are investing capital into the property and seeking a return on your invested capital, not your tenant, who should have their compensation aligned with the profitability of their business instead of the profitability of the real estate.

In an upmarket, you may see tenants sublease half their space at a premium to use that premium and then offset the rent for the space they retain. This is similar to how a residential investor buys a duplex to have one tenant help pay for their mortgage.

Here you also want to ensure that any sublease negates any option language and negates any ability for the sublessee to sublease the space further.

HOLDOVER

Typically, when a lease is up, the tenant has to sign a new lease or vacate. As we all know, tenants are not always the timeliest with moving out. If you have a tight schedule in remodeling or cleaning up the space for your next tenant, the existing tenant could cost you quite a bit of money. Holdover language states that the tenant would need to pay the penalty on top of the monthly rent for each additional month they stay in the building beyond their agreement.

Holdovers used to be 110 percent of the rent. Holdover rates increased after the Great Financial Collapse (GFC) to 125 percent to 150 percent. Starting around 2020, the amount has increased to 200 percent. The irony is that in the 2019–2022 portion of the market cycle, industrial rents were going up at such a fast clip that a tenant who signed a lease in 2017 that expired in 2022 was now so far under the market that 200 percent of rent was just the new rent, not a penalty. In that case, the tenant still doesn't have the right to stay month to month, but given that the holdover rent was no more than market rent, the penalty mechanism was greatly deflated.

Most do not have the operating expenses subject to holdover, but more aggressive landlords do. The devil is in the details here. If the operating expenses are defined as additional rent, and the holdover language states that all additional rent is subject to holdover, then both the rent and operating expenses shall be subject to that penalty. I used to think that this was usury. However, one must consider that it is impractical to calculate the damage to the landlord associated with holding over, much less the court costs and effort to collect on any judgment.

KEY TAKEAWAYS

- Leases must account for a long-term relationship, often ten years, and prepare for many possible scenarios within that time frame.
- Form contracts, like those provided by AIR, can save time and money by providing prewritten, standardized agreements representing balanced interests.
- The landlord's attorney typically draws up custom contracts and can be more suited to specific real estate needs but may require more time and resources.
- Prologis's Clear Lease is an example of a shorter, simpler lease that still offers robust protections for both parties.
- Choosing the right attorney is crucial. They should be empathetic, responsive, and focus on high-impact work. Avoid those with big egos or poor communication habits.
- It's important to ensure the legal entity listed in the lease agreement is valid and licensed to do business in the state where the property is located.
- The lease should include a disclaimer regarding the approximation of square footage to avoid potential disputes over rent.
- Important dates that should be clarified in a lease agreement include the Rent Commencement Date, Operating Expenses Date, Early Possession Date, Possession Date, and Drop-Dead Date.
- The amount due upon the execution of the lease must be clearly defined, and the lease should not be signed until the payment has cleared.
- Free-rent provisions must be clear, indicating which months will be abated and specifying whether or not operating expenses are abated during this period.

- Security deposits should never be used as the last month's rent. Landlords should consider asking for an enhanced security deposit to protect against risk.
- Expenses for maintenance, repair, and replacement should be explicitly outlined in the lease, identifying who is responsible for which items.
- Include profit-sharing provisions in your sublease section language to discourage tenants from seeking profit through subleasing and to ensure the landlord shares in potential profits from subleasing.
- Increase holdover rates to 200 percent of rent or at least have them increase to 200 percent if the tenant holdover is longer than ninety days.
- Are your operating expenses subject to holdover? They can be. If you want them to be, make sure the lease is explicit about this.

NEXT STEPS

You now have a deal in hand and a drafted lease. Now it's time to customize that lease to ensure it includes any scenarios outside the norm. Think of these as add-on clauses that can provide further protections for special situations.

CHAPTER 10

ADDENDUMS, WORK LETTERS, AND EXHIBITS

ADDENDUMS, WORK LETTERS, AND EXHIBITS ARE THE fine- tuning of lease contracts. We have these documents to cover all of the specialized situations we often deal with as business owners and as the economy evolves. It is prevalent to be halfway through a lease with a landlord-tenant issue that needs resolving only to discover that the concern in question wasn't addressed in the lease. This is how the six-page lease of the 1990s is the thirty-page lease of 2023.

AMERICANS WITH DISABILITIES ACT

The landlord is responsible for having a building conforming to ADA standards and codes when the initial building was built. If a tenant needs to modify their space, they will then be responsible for retrofitting the space to the newest standards of ADA based on their use of the building.

ADA upgrades can be costly, so it is imperative to know what does and doesn't trigger upgrades and to be very cognizant of the tenant's use and what part of the tenant's use might trigger upgrades. You will be responsible for common-area upgrades in most instances.

The city usually won't make you update the building in every instance. The mechanism of ADA is often triggered when you pull permits for construction, and the result is usually that the quantity of ADA improvements necessitated will be proportionate to the contract amount of the construction being contemplated.

The tenant's insurance can also cover ADA claims, including the right to select the counsel to defend your interests.

GUARANTOR

This is the legal entity that guarantees financial obligations if the tenant defaults. Language in the agreement must state that the guarantor is stepping into the tenant's shoes if things go south.

Suppose the tenant is a subsidiary of the guarantor. In that case, there is a chance that the parent company will sell the subsidiary/tenant and no longer be the guarantor affiliated with the property.

An industrial guarantor is similar to a parent cosigning their child's first car purchase. Only in commercial real estate is the guarantor a parent company. The entity might be a local air conditioning company, while the guarantor is General Electric, their parent company.

Why is this information important? This allows you to check that the parties have proper licenses (and those licenses are not expired or suspended) to conduct business in your building. Otherwise, the lease may not be valid, and you could suffer unexpected vacancies that lessen operating income.

You may look at a lease with a false sense of security and think, "Fantastic! General Electric is the guarantor, and there is no risk of not receiving the full lease contract amount." You fail to realize that back-out language exists in many lease agreements. Often, there is language in the lease that states that if the entity's business is sold, the guarantor is null and void.

Do your due diligence and discover any sunsetting language in the agreement. The term "sunsetting" refers to the expiration of something part of the way through the contract. For example, you sign a ten-year lease with a corporate guarantee, but the guarantee only applies for the first five years. This could change how you, and the market, view a property's value.

MOVE-OUT CONDITION

Just as tenants want their buildings in good condition when they move in, landlords want buildings in good condition when they get them back. As mentioned in chapter 2, recently, language has been cropping up in leases that reflects move-out conditions as part of a push-and-pull conversation about expectations for property upkeep and use.

Here is sample language to consider:

> Before surrendering the Premises, Tenant shall remove all of its personal property, trade fixtures, and such improvements, alterations, or additions (collectively, "Tenant Additions") to the Premises made by Tenant as may be specified for removal by Landlord and shall repair any damage caused by such removal such that the damaged area returns to the condition that existed before the installation of such Tenant Additions. Tenant shall, at its sole cost and expense, engage a consultant acceptable to the Landlord to oversee the removal if it is deemed necessary by the Landlord, in its sole discretion. Ordinary wear and tear shall not include any damage or the deterioration that good maintenance practices would have prevented, Tenant's proper and orderly occupation and use of the Premises, or by Tenant's timely obligations in this Lease.
>
> If the Tenant fails to remove the Tenant Additions upon the Expiration Date or earlier termination of this Lease, the same shall be deemed abandoned and shall become the property of the Landlord. Notwithstanding the preceding, Tenant shall be liable to Landlord for all costs and damages incurred by Landlord in removing, storing, or selling such Tenant Additions and restoring the Premises to the condition required as provided in this Lease.
>
> Notwithstanding anything to the contrary in this Lease and in addition to the requirements of Paragraph 6.4 of the Lease, the Tenant shall surrender the Premises, at the time of the Expiration Date or earlier termination of this Lease, in a condition that shall include, without limitation, the following:

1. Lights: Office, warehouse, and exterior lights and ballasts must be fully operational with all bulbs functioning. Replace broken light lenses with matching lenses. Ballast color should all be uniform (either all "cool" or all "warm").

2. Dock Levelers & Roll-Up Doors: Must be fully operational. Damaged panels must be replaced and painted to match. Replace all missing or damaged dock bumpers, dock levelers, Dok-loks, and Dok-lok lights.

3. Truck Doors, Dock Seals, and Awnings: Metal and fabric awnings must be free of damage and tears. Frames and fasteners must be secure and undamaged. Dock seals must be free of damage, operational, and securely fastened in place.

4. Warehouse Floors and Columns: Must be free of stains and swept with no racking bolts and other protrusions left on the floor. Bolts must be ground down or removed and patched with an appropriate epoxy filling; remove bolts with a gas torch. Repair cracks in the floor that are ¼" or greater with an epoxy sealer. Reseal any heavily scarred floor seal. Repair damaged or bent columns, bollards, railing, etc.

5. Tenant Installed Equipment & Wiring: Must be removed and space returned to original condition when leased (remove air lines, junction boxes, conduit, etc.). Security systems must be disarmed and removed with damage, if any, repaired. Remove phone systems and damage, if any.

6. Walls: All nails, shelves, and toggle bolts must be removed from walls. Holes must be professionally filled and sanded. Large damaged areas may require tape, bed, and sanding. Holes must not remain in either office or warehouse walls. Remove any sticky residue from placards or signs.

7. Roof: Remove any Tenant-installed equipment and have roof penetrations properly repaired by a licensed roofing contractor approved by Landlord. If roof maintenance is a Tenant's responsibility, then fix active leaks, and complete the most

recent Landlord maintenance and repairs recommendations by a licensed roofing contractor approved by Landlord.

8. Signs: Remove all exterior Tenant signage, patch holes, fixings, and remediate and touch up paint to match, as necessary. Remove all door and window signs, and repair damage, if any.

9. Heating & Air Conditioning System: If maintenance of the HVAC equipment is a Tenant's responsibility, then submit a written report from a licensed contractor to the Landlord within the last two (2) months of the Term. The report must (i) state that all evaporative coolers and heaters within the warehouse are operational and safe and that the office HVAC system is also in good and safe operating condition, and (ii) set out detailed specifications of work necessary to put any equipment and installations into such condition. Complete all repairs/maintenance specified in the HVAC report by Tenant.

10. Painting: All touch-up painting must match the existing paint. Fully repaint scarred and damaged walls and rooms.

11. Doors: All interior and exterior personnel doors (for office and warehouse) must be in good appearance and fully operational, including fixtures, door closers, etc. Holes/scars in doors must be repaired and painted to match. Irreparable holes will require door replacement of matching and like-quality doors. Any signs or name placards on doors must be removed, and any residue leftover from adhesion.

12. Ceiling Tiles: Replace any damaged or stained ceiling tiles in the office.

13. Overall Cleanliness: Clean windows, kitchens, and restrooms to full janitorial standard (i.e., strip/wax floors, sanitize toilets and sinks, clean under cabinets, exhaust fans must be operational, fixtures must be operational, etc.), professionally clean carpet, VCT floors require stripping and waxing, and remove all debris from office and warehouse areas. Remove

all pallets and debris from the exterior of the Premises. Do not temporarily store debris and trash outside of the Building. The parking lot must be swept and the dumpster removed. If appropriate, interior pest control treatment must be completed.

14. Building Systems: All building systems must be in good and safe working order (e.g., plumbing, electrical, fire alarms, intruder alarms, etc.). Provide certification of recent fire sprinkler inspection by a licensed company if a Tenant is responsible.

15. External: All landscaping, parking, and other external areas must be repaired as necessary if a Tenant's responsibility, including, without limitation, the removal of all debris and trash, remarking/repainting parking lots, repair/replacement of generic and emergency signage, resetting/replacing damaged curb stones, and replacing/repairing damaged gully grids and maintenance hole covers.

16. Upon Completion: Contact the Landlord's property manager to coordinate the date of turning off power and utilities, turning in keys, and obtaining the final Landlord Inspection of the Premises.

OPTION TO EXTEND/RENEW

Options are one-way rights for the tenant to stay in the property. For landlords, options to extend are like kryptonite. The general rule is don't give options to anybody anywhere, anytime, unless you have to. If you include one, ask for something in return, and don't do it lightly.

The value of your property is tied to the tenant's lease agreement terms and can make it much more challenging to sell the property because you will have to choose the timing of the sale of the property based on your tenant's option rather than when it is optimal for you.

Most option language includes "baseball arbitration." This is where two brokers or appraisers will collaboratively hire an independent third party to determine the fair market value.

Here's the twist. Whatever fair market value this third party decides as the fair market value *is not* what is paid. This FMV assessment is merely the mechanism to select the winner. Let's say the tenant wants to pay one dollar, but you (the landlord) want to charge two dollars. If the third party determines the fair value is one dollar and fifty-one cents, the final price will be two dollars. If the value is determined to be one dollar and forty-nine cents, the final price will be only one dollar. That creates a scenario where both parties are disincentivized from creating an unrealistic fair market value before the third party steps in.

Some inexperienced landlords will think they can force out a tenant with a renewal option if they unfairly place a high "fair market" value on their property. But, in reality, that rarely happens.

Included in the renewal terms are the dates that act as decision deadlines. Renewals can only be optioned within a specific time frame, usually around six, nine, or twelve months in advance of the end of the lease.

Quite often, tenants forget that they have lease renewal options. If the tenant misses their renewal option deadline, the landlord can negotiate new terms on a rent increase. If they are fixed, waiting to engage your tenant in renewal negotiations is best until their option lapses.

At a minimum, you want the floor to the FMV not to be in an amount less than is currently being charged at the time of the lease option.

You can go one step further and define your option not to allow any leasing concessions prevalent in the market for new tenants, as the concessions given to induce a new tenant to sign a lease are considered irrelevant to an existing tenant looking to continue their lease. Then go one step further and ensure no tenant improvements shall be included in any option to renew.

TENANT IMPROVEMENTS

Tenant improvements are usually described in a work letter exhibit. The key differentiations you need to make are these:

- What is the scope of the work?
- Who is paying for the improvements?
- How much is the allowance?
- Who is in charge of contracting and managing the improvements?
- Who is responsible for cost overruns and change orders?

Tenant improvements are where novice landlords and tenants get themselves into trouble. It happens all the time. Common mistakes include the following:

- The scope of work does not define fixtures, materials, and finishes to be included.
- The parties try to solicit bids from contractors without using an architect to design the space and pricing plan.
- The additional contractor profit, overhead, and contingency are not factored into the amount contemplated for the project.
- There is no thought as to who is responsible for budget overages.
- There are unrealistic timelines for permitting, commencement, and completion.

TIs are easily among the most common places for both parties to be disgruntled. On top of that, it is a terrible way to start a relationship in a spat over construction, as it is hard to recover and turn it into a winning relationship.

- When delivering TIs for the tenant turnkey, always get the overage paid for by the tenant before you contribute your capital to the project.

- When providing tenant improvement allowances, ensure that the funds are only available to reimburse for physical improvements to the premises and any reasonably associated soft costs.
- Even if you are self-managing the TIs, make sure to include your construction management fee unless the tenant is hiring their project manager, and even then, you will still need to oversee your interests in the project.
- Have a detailed requirements list for the disbursement of TI funds, and have a sunset on those funds if they are not used or requested.

Hayes Graham of Terreno perfectly describes how tenant improvements have changed during 2020–2022: "Our tenant improvement language has changed significantly where the landlord will use their best effort to complete the needed construction in a reasonable timeline, but ultimately the lease commencement is no longer tied to completing that work. With lease commencement, you now receive any free rent you've negotiated, and then the rent schedule begins whether the TI is completed or not, with no exceptions. This has been hard for people to understand initially but is now commonplace with widespread delays in construction materials nationwide."

RULES AND REGULATIONS

Rules and regulations are like the HOA rules of the business park the tenant is joining. They include directions for overnight parking, designated parking, signage, trash pickup, and typical rules that govern these properties. Professional landlords will include rules and regulations to set expectations for their tenants, and creating boundaries for good and bad behavior helps set the tone for your professional spaces.

Whereas the language of the rest of the lease is set in stone, the rules and regulations are subject to change as property management adapts to changing needs. Violation of rules and regulations is a default under the lease. You reserve the right even if you do not consistently enforce the rules and regulations. Here are some of the most common rules and regulations that govern tenants' behavior:

- The prohibition of overnight parking of passenger vehicles, tractor-trailers, or containers if it is problematic or inconsistent with how the property is oriented.
- Noise restrictions and hours of operation restrictions for the industrial property directly adjacent to residential property.
- Signage, installation, removal, and style guidelines.

HAZMAT CERTIFICATE

This document is used to gain a thorough understanding and documentation of all of the chemicals the prospective tenant will use, including quantity, location, and storage practices. There may be new information that causes you to reassess your risks with taking on the tenant.

ENVIRONMENTAL, SOCIAL, GOVERNANCE (ESG)

The function of ESG in a lease differs for everyone. As landlords must become more environmentally and socially conscious in how their building is used, those requirements have begun to be built into lease agreements. A relatively common form of ESG would be to include language stating that tenants must use recycled materials for tenant improvements when practical. I've also seen traffic mitigation language to lessen the number of trucks making trips to and from a property. On the social side, that might mean the tenant must do a certain percentage of business with minority-owned or veteran-owned businesses to bolster historically disadvantaged groups. Or, it could be mandating the use of union labor.

ESG is gaining steam, so intentionally shape your policy based on your company's mission and values.

SIGNATORIES

Signatories are the specific people authorized to sign the lease. When signing on the dotted line, you must ensure the right people are doing the signing.

Many states mandate that two corporate officers sign contracts, like in Florida. Others require both husband and wife to sign the lease if a married person is signing personally.

What is most important is to confirm that the person signing the lease is authorized to do so. The mechanism for many tenants is the corporate resolution document. An officer provides this document, which gives the designated signer the authority to sign for the corporation. This is good to ask for if there is any doubt about the signatory's authority.

LEASE SIGNING PROTOCOL

A strict process occurs before the lease is signed by the landlord. To fully execute the lease, there needs to be a stipulation: you will receive the lease signed by the tenant and their check. Next, you will cash the check and ensure it clears. Only after the money has changed hands will you sign the lease.

There are many war stories of doing this process out of order and the headache-inducing legal battles that follow. Don't add your own experiences to that fold. The perfect world for you as a landlord is to set up an electronic signature and ACH payment to handle everything digitally and promptly.

CLOSING OUT

Closing out a lease includes cashing the check and signing the lease, but before you give your tenant the keys, there are some things to wrap up.

Mainly, you need to receive the tenant's certificate of insurance. Worrisomely, only around 75 percent are done correctly. The other 25 percent will include terms and stipulations that are not what you agreed to in the lease. Then you must go back and work through amending and adjusting it with their insurance provider.

With the insurance certificate in hand, congratulations! You've successfully closed a lease agreement! Assuming the space is complete, you can give the tenant possession and present them with their keys.

KEY TAKEAWAYS

- If you have an older property, you should have an ADA upgrade plan in mind. This will help you contextualize any construction projects or legal liability that needs to be managed.
- Dial in your move-out condition requirements to ensure the property will be in first-class condition when returned to you at the end of the lease.
- Option to extend/renew lease can impact property value and sale timing.
- "Baseball arbitration" can be inserted to determine fair market value for lease renewals in order to keep both parties from making unreasonable FMV assertions.
- Scope of work, payment, allowance, management, and responsibility for cost overruns should be addressed in TIs.
- Common mistakes in TIs include unclear scope of work, inadequate planning, and unrealistic timelines.
- TI disputes will damage landlord-tenant relationships.
- Ensure proper management of TI funds, and include a sunset clause for unused funds.

- Set expectations for tenants, including parking, signage, and trash pickup, subject to change as property management adapts to changing needs.
- Follow a strict lease signing protocol, including receipt of all monies due before executing the lease and validating the certificate of insurance and then tendering possession of the building.

NEXT STEPS

Congratulations, you have a signed lease, check, and certificate of insurance in your hands! There is nothing sweeter than this moment. This is where the bulk of the cash flow and value is created. As my colleague Scott Smith, principal in our Phoenix office, would counsel, "Don't go to the Porsche dealership just yet." Well, perhaps you can at least make an appointment at the Porsche dealership. For now, there are a few loose ends to tie up: constructing TIs, transitioning the tenant to property management, setting up a payment in the system, and figuring out your next priority with the property. Exciting!

CHAPTER 11

TENANT IMPROVEMENTS AND ONGOING MANAGEMENT

CONGRATULATIONS. YOU NOW HAVE A FULLY EXE-
cuted lease, all monies due, and a certificate of insurance naming
you additionally insured. If you have made it to this point, you have
that new tenant that you've been looking for whom you can build
a relationship and growth with and who will provide cash flow, a
return on your investment, and the increase in the value to the
property that you envisioned when you first acquired it.

Now what? It's time to transition your relationship to property
management, who will be the main point of contact for the tenant for
most of the rest of the time the tenant is within the property. There
are a whole host of details to ensure a smooth transition. This will
now free you up to focus on your next pursuit, whether it be leasing
another of your properties, refinancing to pull out money to invest in
another property, putting your newly leased property on the market
for sale as a leased investment, or going fishing in Mexico!

A fully leased property gives you options to pursue your next goal
and enjoy the cash flow. Here we'll cover that transition, discuss
some of the ongoing management you'll want to review with your
property manager each year, and give you some fresh ideas for what
you can do with your fully leased property.

TRANSITION TO PROPERTY MANAGEMENT

Great property managers will meet the tenant at the building to
introduce themselves. They will be spending even more time with
your new tenant than you and your broker did structuring the deal

in the first place. They have 1,825 or 3,650 days together in a five- or ten-year lease.

As Bob Andrews of Centerpoint Properties suggests, one of the first things you should do here, but also in your overall process of managing properties, is "have a great move-in checklist. Once you have owned a property for a few lease cycles, you can establish a solid up-front move-in process with notes, pictures, and signatures from the tenant that acknowledge the move-in condition. This helps you set your baseline for future conversations, where you can focus more on what constitutes wear and tear and regular maintenance."

Next, part of your move-in checklist is to set up ACH payments so your property manager can stop chasing checks in the mail and automate your income stream. ACH isn't perfect, as every year, the amount needs to be increased to the new amount, but that is of minimal inconvenience.

Your property manager then will want to abstract the lease and update whatever property management system they use, like Yardi, so that all records of the monies received, the annual increases, prepaid rent, security deposit, and lease expiration are logged into the system for future accounting. Next, they will want to log the property insurance certificate within their system so that they can quickly verify it each year to ensure it remains valid and in force.

Pay your broker promptly. Remember, your broker has been working for free for months to ensure the outcome you are celebrating. Leasing commissions are due half upon lease signing and half upon possession. Some landlords pay on a net thirty schedule from lease signing. And then, the accounting department should have cut the check that week. Then when the check doesn't arrive on time and can't be found, a stop-issue payment is issued. A new check run comes and goes, and a new check is cut and then goes through the mail system. The broker's office manager then receives the check and has to hold it to clear it before paying their broker. Their broker's bank needs to wait a day to clear the check. The whole while the broker is holding their breath waiting to get paid for six months of work they have done without compensation.

Some landlords pay more. Some pay faster. Some use this as their competitive advantage and have a policy that the broker's check will be at their office within forty-eight hours via FedEx. Some wire funds the same day. Which policy will make the broker work harder? Be the landlord that prides themself on honoring the broker who put the deal together.

ONGOING MANAGEMENT

Time will go by, days will turn into weeks, months, and years, and it soon comes time to adjust. Thankfully, the passage of time is precisely what you are looking for as an investor because every month that goes by is a month of additional cash flow, additional return on your invested capital, increased appreciation based on new higher rental amounts based on annual increases, and so on.

AGING REPORTS

Aging means late payments. Great property managers balance the need to enforce the lease late-payment fees with the need for positive tenant relations and will be understanding when there are fluke instances. Being too loose is not ideal but not uncommon, but being too strict is a surefire way to have your tenant base itching to move out upon lease expiration. Here you have to make sure that you nip problems in the bud and enforce the lease so that you protect your interests. Much like health problems are best known early so you can be proactive toward a solution, so are late payments.

CAM RECONCILIATIONS

There is almost always some form of common area maintenance (CAM) reconciliation that must occur unless you have a single-tenant absolute net lease or you have gross leases with no pass-throughs whatsoever. In single-tenant absolute net leases, the tenant takes care of the property as if they owned it, and they pay the property tax bill and maintain, repair, and replace anything needed, including the roof, the load-bearing walls, and the foundation. In a multi-tenant gross lease, the tenant only pays the rent, no matter how much it costs to operate the business park. Both are the minority of instances.

Most triple net and modified gross leases either have an estimated operating expense that needs to be trued up each year or have a base year pass-through of costs that can be billed to the tenant after truing up all payments. Don't miss this opportunity.

Mom-and-pops, and even many high-net-worth investors, don't know or don't take the time to do this because they are unaware and perceive it to be too complicated or too time intensive. Consider CAM reconciliations as a thirteenth lease payment in the twelve-month calendar year. What investor wouldn't want that?

What is involved in CAM reconciliations? You need to know:

- The total twelve-month property expenses
- The property expense budget
- The specific property expenses that are reimbursable per the lease agreements
- The number of reimbursable expenses from the prior calendar year
- The proportionate amount of costs the tenant is responsible for
- The tenant's base year if there is one

With the lease in hand, as well as the year-end property management report, and last year's accounting, your property manager can start to estimate if any outstanding CAM reconciliations need to be collected.

RENT INCREASES

Believe it or not, landlords miss rent escalations. It may be no surprise that tenants need to pay rent increases. But some do not. Why does this happen? Usually, do-it-yourself landlords miss rent escalations because they need a property management accounting system to keep track of the rent roll. If you missed increasing the rent, you'll want to correct that mistake but will likely find it challenging to collect on a large lump sum of back rent. Usually, these mistakes are rectified over time or wrapped into a new longer-term lease deal. Don't be that landlord!

PROPERTY TAXES

Your property tax bill will be the most considerable annual expense you have associated with the property. As a result, you likely remember exactly how much it is to the dollar.

Certain counties or municipalities have different property tax assessments for floating valuations. Some have annual maximum caps, while other municipalities evaluate property taxes annually. For floating valuations, landlords can protest the tax. Subsequently, a cottage industry of tax protest companies works on contingency.

New forms of taxes are also emerging in different areas of the country. In Florida, an occupancy tax is charged to the landlord to bill the tenant. California has a clean air tax similar to the occupancy tax. Los Angeles instituted a "mansion tax" of 5.5 percent of the sale proceeds for properties over $10 million. In Texas, a margin tax passes through to the tenant. Great property managers know the local nuances of any taxes related to the property they manage.

There is room for property tax values to get bungled. It is rare, but there is the infrequent occasion where properties have the incorrect tax rates applied without the landlord knowing. In one instance, I worked on a distribution property in San Antonio, Texas, that Bexar County had incorrectly labeled as a flex building, which increased its property tax by 50 percent. A seasoned property manager will catch this error and save the landlord and, in most instances, the tenant tens of thousands of dollars.

Tax protests are prevalent in Texas and a handful of other states. These take place when you hire a consultant on a contingency fee basis to protest your property tax amount and then they share in the savings with you often on a 75/25 or 80/20 basis. During market fluctuations and times of need for municipalities to raise revenue, a property tax protest can be a worthy endeavor.

The key thing to remember with property taxes is to factor them into the structuring of your lease. You will likely be starting a new lease during the middle of a property tax cycle, so you want to ensure you are correctly calculating the amount to bill back to the tenant. Take an extra moment to verify this.

TENANT CERTIFICATES OF INSURANCE

You might be surprised that your tenant no longer has an active general liability policy listing you as additionally insured. Tenants sometimes switch insurance companies during the course of the lease. When there is an insurance company change, there is the opportunity for COIs to be done improperly and without additional insurance covering the landlord. Great property managers request updated COIs every year.

PROPERTY INSURANCE

Your property insurance is subject to renewal each year. Most industrial landlords who are keeping an eye on their property insurance have noticed significant premium increases due to weather or environmental effects, whether it be earthquakes in California, hurricanes in Florida, tornadoes in Tennessee, freezing temperatures and electrical grid failures in Texas, fires in Washington, etc.

Even though there is an 80 percent chance that your policy is either Travelers or Hartford insurance, you will still find it worth it to bid out your insurance policy each year to multiple carriers.

Look for ways to combine policies with carriers, adjust your premiums and coverage, and always use your annual renewal as a time to adjust and optimize.

SUBLEASES

If you play the property ownership game long enough, you will have a tenant that no longer needs their space and will sublease it to a new tenant. Your lease should allow this only with your knowledge, review, and consent.

Most leases will tell you that the lease is terminated if your tenant subleases the property without your approval. It is a massive no-no in commercial real estate leasing. We have worked through a few of these and can verify that they usually leave everyone with a bad taste in their mouths. The company that did the unauthorized sublease is now in the lurch to the new tenant and in default of their lease with their landlord. You are unhappy that you have not vetted some unknown tenant in your property to be safe, clean, and legal. And lastly, the company that is the new unauthorized tenant is unhappy because they were promised they could use the space, and they can try to sue the tenant that leased it to them. This is not fun, profitable, or sustainable for either of the three parties.

Most landlords aggressively assert control over the property and ensure they are protected. It might be preferable if the use is benign and the sublessee's financials check out. In a strong market, you likely will want to take the space back to bump the rent and profit from the delta between the contract and market rent amounts. In a down market, however, you may be better off keeping the sublessee as it is better than no lessee, and there are now two tenants on the hook responsible for making sure the rent is paid.

BUDGETING

Not all property managers proactively budget. Institutional investors, operators, and syndicators have fiduciary responsibilities to their investors, making budgeting a nonnegotiable. Consider it a nonnegotiable no matter what size your property is. Put property budgeting on your calendar for September 1. Attack it early if you have a portfolio or complex holdings. Delay it a month or two if you are at capacity and out of bandwidth. But do it. All budgeting exercises are worth it. This is where you will brainstorm future opportunities to increase revenue and predict one-time expenses before they become surprises.

Go back to chapter 2 and walk through the Set a Baseline exercise. The more you go through this process for each property, the better assumptions you will make, and the better cash flow and capital gains you will produce with consistency.

LEASING LIFE CYCLE

This completes the life cycle of the industrial leasing process. Many of you do this daily with your portfolios, like tying your shoes in the morning. For those advanced-level investors, I have added some tips and tricks for you to add to your repertoire to produce superior returns.

For those of you who only go through the leasing process occasionally, I want you to have a step-by-step guide you can rely on to conceptually get you from the starting gate to the finish line. This will help you work with your team, broker, tenant, and the rest of the commercial real estate industry to produce high-level results even with limited daily experience.

KEY TAKEAWAYS

- Utilize a move-in checklist to document property conditions and establish a baseline.
- Abstract the lease and update property management systems with lease details.
- Pay brokers promptly to maintain positive relationships.

- Monitor aging reports to manage late payments and maintain positive tenant relations.
- Conduct CAM reconciliations to recover expenses.
- Ensure timely rent increases according to the lease.
- Monitor property taxes and local nuances, and protest if necessary.
- Regularly update tenant certificates of insurance and property insurance.
- Manage subleases with tenant consent and ensure protection for landlords.
- Implement proactive budgeting for property management and expenses.

NEXT STEPS

What will you do now that you have a handle on leasing your industrial assets? If you are like me, you will celebrate for all of two minutes and work through a quick assessment of what worked, what didn't, and what improvements you can make the next time. Then it is time to move on to your next adventure, where you will figure out how to use this experience to create something new and wonderful.

CONCLUSION

IF YOU HAVE READ *LETTERS FROM A STOIC* BY SENECA, **you will** enjoy that the entire book is written in the form of a letter from Seneca to one of his friends, Lucilius. Each letter is a lesson telling a story about an experience and how it can instruct his friend to be a better Stoic.

Seneca always reflects at the end of the letter and makes sure that the letter makes good on its promise to leave his friend with practical advice. This conclusion is where I make good on my promise to you. I promised to give you a framework to think through your industrial leasing, a step-by-step guide, guidance on avoiding pitfalls, and strategies and tactics for adding cash flow and property value to your industrial properties.

Looking back on this manuscript, we have covered a lot of ground together.

We started by sizing up and understanding the property and tenant trends in the marketplace so that you could begin any assignment with a fundamental understanding of the world you are about to enter.

We then transitioned to the specific property that you are about to work on and looked at it from a 360-degree perspective so that you can get a holistic view of the job in front of you.

From there, we talked through who the players are on the fields and how to think through how time affects you and your tenants and the future construction and negotiation that is about to take place.

We then thought through how to assess whether keeping your current tenant or finding a new one is better and how to proceed along a parallel path so that you remain in a good position no matter your chosen direction.

After that, we discussed how to pick the best broker for you, your property, and the leasing assignment at hand. After selecting your broker, we helped you determine what parts of the listing agreement warrant your attention.

We dove into the marketplace and started looking at what makes the ideal tenant for you and gave you a lens through which you can evaluate and negotiate with prospective tenants.

We also took out the financial microscope and inspected every facet of the tenant and lease financials to draw insight into the value the tenant is providing you.

We transitioned into the lease contract clauses to custom-tailor the lease to suit your needs.

We even spent an extra chapter fine-tuning the lease contract to ensure it has every additional protection you might need.

From there, we celebrated your new tenant by transitioning them to your property management team and setting the stage for your next move.

I'm amazed at how many books' worth of material was left on the cutting room floor. At one point, I thought I might cover the acquisitions and disposition process within the same manuscript. I thought I could cover the ins and outs of construction and tenant improvements. I thought I could delve into the most valuable aspects of asset and property management. I contemplated delving into property financing as it is outsized in many investors' properties. But each of these topics is vast, and I found that I had to do justice to the work that I knew would create the most value to you, and deep down, I knew that it was the leasing process. Thankfully, there are plenty of opportunities for more writing to share with you.

With the insider's knowledge of the leasing process, you can now elevate your portfolio, improve upon it, and drive value for decades. Effective leasing will help you acquire properties better. It will help you develop properties better. It will help you position your properties for maximum value better.

Please share your feedback on this body of work, whether good, bad, or ugly, as all feedback helps me understand what does and does not work for the reader and to improve future releases.

Other than providing feedback, the biggest thing I can ask of you, the reader, is to collaborate with me and my team. We are always looking for great people to brainstorm with, to interview on our podcast, and to create new opportunities to make our collective pipelines as robust as possible.

Connect with me on Linkedin at
www.linkedin.com/in/justinbsmith/

Follow me on Instagram at
www.instagram.com/industrialsmith/

Listen to our podcast at
podcasts.apple.com/us/podcast/industrial-insights/
id1552731790/

Keep current on our team's capabilities at
smithcre.com

And best of all, shoot me an email at
jbsmith@leeirvine.com

Let's go!

ACKNOWLEDGMENTS

I COULD HAVE DONE A BETTER JOB ACKNOWLEDGING people who contributed to my success in *Industrial Intelligence*. I want to correct that and recognize those who have helped contribute to my success and who took the time to help make this specific project the best it could be.

For my family who supported me along my journey: Lindsay, Emmeline, and Annabelle Smith, Brian & LaVonne Smith (AKA, Mom & Dad, Nana & Papa), Don & Jane Sullivan (AKA Ama and Apa), Sammy Smith, Gina Jacobson, Kevin Claire, and Lily, Tony & Sara Bolliger, Owen, Max, Theo, and Baby Ben, Gary & Amanda Thompson, Augustus, and Eli.

For all those who took a chance on me: Guy LaFerrara, Mike Baker, Dale Camera, Scott Smith, David Newton, Dave Fister, Greg Maher, Brad Vetter, John Curtis, Grant LaBounty, and Chris Vassilian.

For all those who contributed to this writing endeavor: Everybody at the Scribe Media team, Lisa Shiroff, Eliece Pool, Ami Hendrickson, Hal Clifford, Christina Taylor, Anton Khodakovsky, Jeannette Cano, Jim Clewlow, Shawn Clark, Graham Wahlberg, Carlos Serra, Bill Shopoff, Bob Thiergartner, Nicole Welch, Joonas Partanen, Devin Barnwell, Jim Camp, Emma Miller, Jenny Garcia, Bob Andrews, Jeff Won, DeVonne Boler, Matthew Reynolds, Hayes Graham, Matt Ehrlich, John Quinn, Mike Calhoun, Craig Yocum, Sebastian Espinosa, John Cassidy, Jack Cline, Chris Petersen, Mike Tingus, Craig Viergever, John Feinberg, Jason Baxter.

For those that provided research and market data to bring the marketplace to light: Prologis and Hickey & Associates.

And for those I unintentionally missed, may you know that I love and appreciate you!